P9-BIP-195

The Blender Cookbook

The Blender Cookbook

By

ANN SERANNE

And

EILEEN GADEN

Photographic Illustrations by the Authors

DOUBLEDAY & COMPANY, INC.

GARDEN CITY, NEW YORK

ISBN: 0-385-07978-8
Library of Congress Catalog Card Number 61-11228

Printed in the United States of America
25 24 23 22

Introduction

In the past few years, new techniques have been developed which make an electric blender a necessary part of every modern kitchen.

We are not going to begin by a long discourse on how to use your electric blender, or go into great details as to what your blender will or will not do. Suffice it to say that if you have never used an electric blender before, you will learn quickly by using this book. If you have only used your blender to mix drinks and make soups, you will find within these pages exciting new ideas, short cuts, and magic recipes that will take the drudgery out of cooking and make it a pleasure. If you own an electric blender and have it stored away on a top shelf, get it down! You don't know the treasure you are hiding! Attach it to the handiest electric outlet and *keep* it there. And begin, right away, to make some of the easy and quick recipes —all delicious—in this book. Soon you will find that you will use your blender many times every day in the preparation of your daily meals, to grind, grate, crumb, purée, chop, aerate, and homogenize. Your entire cooking habits will become revolutionized almost overnight. You'll find yourself relegating much of your obsolete, old-fashioned kitchen equipment to that top shelf!

Every recipe in this book has been kitchen tested and is designed to utilize the electric blender to its fullest capacity. Just remember one thing. Your electric blender is a precision appliance. So treat it with the consideration it deserves. Do NOT overwork the motor with too heavy a load; do not expect it to do *everything*. There is not much it cannot do, and what it does do, it does to perfection.

HAPPY BLENDING

Ann Seranne and Eileen Gaden

All recipes tested and all photographs taken in the offices of Seranne and Gaden.

Table of Contents

The Blender Cookbook

PATÉ
FROMAGE
JAMBON

Chapter 1 DIPS, SANDWICH SPREADS, AND BUTTERS

The liquefying action of the electric blender quickly transforms semi-solids such as cheese, nuts, chicken livers, and hard-cooked eggs into a smooth, flavorful dip to serve with crackers, potato chips, or an arrangement of crisp, raw vegetables. A small amount of liquid such as cream, sour cream, mayonnaise, lemon juice, tomato juice, or chicken broth must be used to moisten the semi-solids so the blender can purée them. If you wish a dip with a coarse texture, add small amounts of raw green pepper, scallions, nuts, or olives to the purée just a second or two before turning off the motor, letting them blend just long enough to be chopped into small pieces.

In making thick purées, avoid overworking the motor. Should the vortex cease to draw the mixture down into the blades, either stop the motor and stir the mixture with a *rubber* spatula, or remove cover and, with the motor on, work the surface of the mixture with the rubber spatula, drawing it from the sides of the container into the center. In this way air will be introduced and the vortex will be re-formed. If not, it means that the mixture is too thick and you must add a little more liquid. Add it a tablespoon at a time. Be careful not to dip the spatula too deeply into the purée, and never use a *metal* spoon or spatula.

The following recipes are only a few of the interesting cocktail savories that your blender can make. Use whatever leftover cooked meat, chicken, or fish you have on hand. Add a little liquid, a thin slice of onion or garlic, a favorite herb or seasoning, and you have created your own cocktail specialty.

Basic Cheese Dip

¼ cup water or milk
8 ounces cottage cheese
6 ounces cream cheese
2 ounces blue cheese
1 clove garlic
Few drops Tabasco

In making a smooth mixture such as a purée or dip, always start with enough liquid to cover the blades, or about ¼ cup. The liquid may be water, milk, consommé, tomato juice, et cetera, depending on what is being made. Here we use water or milk.

Add cottage cheese.

Cover container, turn motor on high speed, and blend for 20 seconds. (This mixture makes an excellent substitute for sour cream, with the simple addition of a little lemon juice and salt. It's low-calorie, too.)

Add cream cheese, blue cheese, garlic, and the Tabasco. Cover, turn motor on high speed, and blend for about 10 seconds, or until mixture is smooth.

If vortex ceases to form in a heavy mixture such as a dip or spread, remove cover and carefully break surface with a rubber spatula, pulling mixture from sides of container into center. This will introduce air and the vortex will be re-created. Be careful not to dip the spatula in too deeply.

Makes 1 pint of creamy-smooth dip for vegetable sticks or crackers.

DIPS

Avocado Dip

Into container put

2 avocados, peeled, seeded, and sliced
2 tablespoons lemon juice
4 tablespoons olive oil
1 clove garlic
1 tablespoon chives or green-onion tops
1 teaspoon salt
1 teaspoon dill weed
Dash hot pepper sauce

Cover and blend on high speed until smooth, stopping to stir down if necessary. Store in refrigerator until ready to serve. Makes 1 pint.

Avocado-Cheese Dip

Into container put

½ cup creamy cottage cheese
½ cup mayonnaise
1 tablespoon lemon juice
1 small slice onion
½ teaspoon salt
¼ teaspoon pepper

Cover and blend on high speed for 20 seconds. Remove cover and, with motor on, drop in

1 large avocado, peeled, seeded, and sliced

Empty into bowl. Fold in ¼ cup chopped stuffed olives. Makes 1¾ cups.

Blue-Cheese Dip

Into container put

1 cup creamy cottage cheese
4 ounces blue cheese, crumbled
⅓ cup cream
¼ small onion
1 teaspoon Worcestershire sauce
⅛ teaspoon red pepper
6 sprigs parsley

Cover and blend on high speed until smooth, stopping to stir down if necessary. Makes 1¾ cups.

Cheddar-Beer Dip

Into container put

8 ounces cream cheese
½ cup beer

Cover and blend on high speed for 8 seconds. Add

¼ cup beer
8 ounces Cheddar cheese, cubed
1 clove garlic

Cover and blend for 20 seconds, or until smooth. Add

12 small gherkins
1 teaspoon poppy seeds

Cover and blend for 2 seconds only. Makes 3 cups.

Cheddar-Port Dip

Into container put

⅓ cup port or sherry
⅓ cup cream
1 tablespoon cut chives or green-onion tops
8 ounces sharp Cheddar, diced

Cover and blend on high speed for 40 seconds, or until smooth, stopping to stir down if necessary. Chill. Makes 1½ cups.
May be pressed out onto crackers through a fluted tube if chilled for 2 hours. Also excellent to pack in small crocks. Store in refrigerator.

Clam Dip

Into container put

1 7½-ounce can minced clams, drained
¼ cup liquor from clams
6 ounces cream cheese
¼ teaspoon salt
1 tablespoon cut chives or green-onion tops
6 drops Tabasco
6 sprigs parsley

Cover and blend on high speed for 10 seconds, or until smooth, stopping to stir down if necessary. Chill. Makes 1¼ cups.

Crab-Meat Dip

Into container put

- ⅓ cup cream
- 2 teaspoons lemon juice
- 1 teaspoon Worcestershire sauce
- ¼ teaspoon salt
- Freshly ground pepper
- Small slice garlic clove
- 8 ounces cream cheese

Cover and blend on high speed for 10 seconds. Add

- 1 cup flaked crab meat

Cover and blend for 20 seconds longer, stopping to stir down if necessary. Makes 2 cups.

Curry Dip

Of a thin consistency, delicious to serve as a dip with raw vegetables. Fairly spicy.

Into container put

- 8 ounces cottage cheese
- ½ cup water-cress leaves
- 1 green onion, sliced
- 1 medium tomato, cut in pieces
- ¼ teaspoon salt
- 1½ teaspoons curry powder

Cover and blend on high speed for 30 seconds, stopping to stir down if necessary. Makes 1¾ cups.

Dip Oleh

In small saucepan, heat to boiling

- 1 can *garbanzos* or kidney beans, drained
- ½ cup juice from beans or tomato juice
- 3 tablespoons tomato paste
- 4 to 6 canned hot chili peppers, stemmed

2 tablespoons salad oil
1 teaspoon salt
1 clove garlic

Empty mixture into container. Add

1 cup diced Cheddar cheese

Cover and blend on high speed for 30 seconds, stopping to stir down if necessary. Pour into a casserole and keep hot. If desired, cover top thickly with crumbled, crisp bacon. Serve on sesame-seed crackers.

Ham Dip

Into container put

¾ cup diced ham
½ small onion, halved
½ cup mayonnaise
1 tablespoon Worcestershire sauce
⅛ teaspoon cloves
⅛ teaspoon nutmeg

Cover and blend on high speed for 60 seconds. Makes 1 cup.

CHICKEN DIP

Use chicken in place of ham. Fold in ¼ cup chopped green olives.

Herb Dip

Into container put

2 tablespoons water
1 tablespoon lemon juice
8 ounces cottage cheese
3 ounces cream cheese, halved

Cover and blend on high speed for 30 seconds. Add

½ teaspoon dry basil
½ teaspoon dry tarragon
½ teaspoon dry parsley
1 teaspoon salt
½ teaspoon dill weed
1 clove garlic

Cover and blend on high speed for 10 seconds. Makes 1½ cups.

Olive-Cheese Dip

(May Be Spread on Toast Squares)

Into container put

8 ounces cottage cheese
3 ounces cream cheese, halved
3 tablespoons lemon juice
¼ teaspoon dry onion flakes
¼ teaspoon paprika

Cover and blend on high speed for 30 seconds. Remove cover and gradually add

1 cup sliced ripe olives

Blend on high speed for 30 seconds longer, stopping to stir down if necessary. Makes 1½ cups.

Salmon Dip

Into container put

¼ cup cream
3 drops Tabasco
1 tablespoon coarsely cut chives or green-onion tops
½ teaspoon dill weed
½ teaspoon paprika
Dash salt and pepper
8 ounces cottage cheese
1 7¾-ounce can salmon, drained

Cover and blend on high speed for 40 seconds, stopping to stir down if necessary. Makes 2 cups.

Smoky-Cheese Dip

Into container put

⅓ cup pineapple juice
¼ teaspoon Worcestershire sauce
6 ounces cream cheese

Cover and blend on high speed for 20 seconds. Add

6 ounces smoky cheese, diced
1 small clove garlic

Cover and blend on high speed for 30 seconds. Chill. Makes 1¾ cups.

SPREADS

There are a great many combinations of cheese, fish, or meat that can be blended into sandwich spreads and butters.

Work with small quantities of ingredients and use a rubber spatula. Either stop the motor, when necessary, to stir the ingredients down, or use the rubber spatula lightly on top of the mixture, being careful not to dip deeply. Chill sandwich spreads and butters thoroughly before spreading on thinly sliced, trimmed bread.

By the addition of extra liquid many of these spreads can be thinned to dip consistency. The butter spreads are not recommended for dips.

Butter itself can be blended from sweet or sour cream, and flavored with garlic or herbs while it is blending. It is the sweetest, freshest butter you ever tasted. (See Butters).

Almond-Marmalade Spread

Into container put

2 tablespoons orange juice
½ cup orange marmalade
6 ounces cream cheese, quartered
½ cup blanched almonds

Cover container and blend on high speed for 20 seconds. Chill. Makes 1½ cups.

Apricot-Nut Spread

Into container put

¾ cup dried apricots, soaked overnight and drained
2 tablespoons apricot liquid

Cover and blend on high speed for 10 seconds. Turn off motor and add

6 ounces cream cheese
½ cup walnuts

Cover and blend on high speed for 30 seconds. Chill. Makes 2¼ cups.

Cocktail Cheese Ball

Into container put

½ cup walnuts

Cover and blend on high speed for 6 seconds, or until nuts are ground. Empty onto waxed paper. Into container put

2 tablespoons warm brandy
½ cup (1 stick) soft butter

Cover and blend on high speed until smooth. Uncover, and, with motor on, add piece by piece,

½ cup crumbled blue cheese
½ cup diced semisoft cheese such as Bel Paese

Blend until smooth, stopping to stir down if necessary. Scrape out onto the ground nuts. Put hands under waxed paper and shape into a ball, coating it with the nuts. Wrap in foil and chill. Serve with thin slices pumpernickel bread.

Chicken Spread

Into container put

¼ cup mayonnaise
2 tablespoons sweet pickle relish
3 drops Tabasco
¼ teaspoon salt
¼ teaspoon tarragon
1 cup cooked diced chicken
1 thin slice small onion
½ cup diced celery

Cover and blend on high speed for 30 seconds, stopping to stir down if necessary. Makes 1¼ cups.

CHICKEN-SALAD SPREAD

Use 1 canned pimiento, quartered, ¼ green pepper, cut into strips, and 1 stalk celery, coarsely cut, in place of the relish and celery in recipe above.

Chicken-Curry Spread

Into container put

½ cup mayonnaise
1 teaspoon curry powder

1 teaspoon salt
½ cup toasted almonds
1 thin slice small onion
1 cup cooked, diced chicken

Cover and blend on high speed for 1 minute, stopping to stir down if necessary. Makes 1½ cups.

Chicken-Liver Spread

Simmer for 5 minutes

¾ pound chicken livers, fresh or defrosted
1 small onion, halved
½ cup chicken stock

Empty mixture, including liquid, into container. Add

½ teaspoon paprika
½ teaspoon curry powder
½ teaspoon salt
1 tablespoon Worcestershire sauce
⅛ teaspoon pepper

Cover and blend. Remove cover and, with motor on high, add chunk by chunk

½ cup (1 stick) butter

Stop to stir down if necessary. Chill. Makes 1 pint.

CHICKEN-LIVER-AND-CREAM-CHEESE SPREAD

Use only ½ pound chicken livers. Add 8 ounces cream cheese instead of the butter.

Crab-Meat Spread

Drain, flake, and discard cartilage from 1 6½-ounce can crab meat. Into container put

½ cup mayonnaise
Juice from ½ lime
1 tablespoon cut chives or green-onion tops
½ teaspoon dry tarragon
1 tablespoon sherry
¼ teaspoon salt
Dash cayenne
The crab meat

Cover and blend on high speed for 20 seconds, stopping to stir down if necessary. Serve on rounds of bread or crackers. Makes 1¼ cups.

Date-Nut Spread

Into container put

¼ cup pineapple juice
Pulp from ½ orange

Cover and blend on high speed for 5 seconds. Add

⅓ cup nuts
¾ cup pitted dates

Cover and blend on high speed for 20 seconds, stopping to stir down when necessary. Chill. Makes 1 cup.

Deviled-Ham Spread

Into container put

1 tablespoon tomato paste
1 teaspoon Worcestershire sauce
1 slice small onion
1 teaspoon sugar
1 4½-ounce can deviled ham
6 parsley sprigs
2 stalks celery, cut up

Cover and blend on high speed for 40 seconds, stopping to stir down if necessary. Chill. Makes 1 cup.

Egg Spread

Into container put

2 tablespoons cream
2 tablespoons mayonnaise
½ teaspoon salt
¼ teaspoon celery salt
Thin slice small onion
3 drops Tabasco

Cover and blend on high speed for 10 seconds. Remove cover and, with motor on, drop in

4 hard-cooked egg yolks

Turn speed to low and drop in

4 hard-cooked egg whites

Turn off motor as soon as whites are coarsely chopped. Makes 1 cup.

Ham-Nut Spread

Into container put

¼ cup mayonnaise
1 cup cooked, diced ham
¼ cup walnuts
¼ teaspoon salt
½ teaspoon dry mustard
1 slice small onion

Cover and blend on high speed for 20 seconds, stopping to stir down. Makes 1 cup.

Olive-Nut Spread

Into container put

2 tablespoons cream or sour cream
8 ounces soft cream cheese
½ cup stuffed olives
¼ cup pecans

Cover and blend for 30 seconds, stopping to stir down if necessary. Makes 1½ cups.

Peanut-Jelly Spread

Into container put

½ cup roasted peanuts
1 tablespoon salad oil

Cover and blend on high speed until peanuts are pureed. Add

¼ cup tart jam or jelly

Cover and blend for 20 seconds, or until mixed, stopping to stir down if necessary. Makes ½ cup.

Salmon Spread

Into container put

¼ cup mayonnaise
1 tablespoon lemon juice
Few drops Tabasco
1 slice small onion
1 stalk celery, cut into pieces
1 7¾-ounce can salmon, drained

Cover and blend on high speed for 20 seconds, stopping to stir down if necessary. Chill. Makes 1¼ cups.

Sardine Spread

Into container put

2 tablespoons mayonnaise
2 teaspoons lemon juice
⅛ teaspoon pepper
1 cup sardines

Cover and blend on high speed for 20 seconds, stopping to stir down if necessary. Makes 1 cup.

Tangy Cheese Spread

Into container put

½ cup cream
1 slice garlic
¼ cup parsley sprigs
1 teaspoon Worcestershire sauce
¼ teaspoon salt
Few drops Tabasco
1 cup diced Cheddar cheese

Cover and blend on high speed for 30 seconds, stopping to stir down if necessary. Makes 1 cup.

Tongue Spread

Into container put

½ cup cooked diced tongue or ham
¼ cup sautéed or canned mushrooms
4 gherkins or 1 small dill pickle
2 tablespoons mayonnaise

Cover and blend on high speed for 30 seconds, stopping to stir down if necessary. Makes about 1 cup.

Tuna Spread

Into container put

½ cup mayonnaise
½ small onion
½ teaspoon salt
¼ teaspoon pepper
1 teaspoon Worcestershire sauce
1 7-ounce can tuna, drained
1 stalk celery, cut in pieces
1 small carrot, cut in pieces

Cover and blend on high speed for 30 seconds. Chill. Makes 1¾ cups.

Water-Cress Spread

Into container put

2 tablespoons cream
Leaves from 1 bunch water cress
1 tablespoon horse-radish
½ teaspoon salt
1 slice garlic clove
8 ounces cream cheese

Cover and blend for 30 seconds, or until smooth. Chill. Makes 1¼ cups.

WATER-CRESS-WALNUT SPREAD

½ cup walnuts may be added during the last 10 seconds.

BUTTERS

An electric blender can make butter from leftover heavy cream, sweet or sour (not commercial sour cream). By adding a clove of garlic during the churning process you have the best garlic butter you ever tasted. Try adding a few sprigs of fresh tarragon or other herb, fresh or dried.

Garlic Butter

Into container put

1 cup heavy cream

Cover and turn motor on high speed. Remove cover and blend until cream is whipped. Add

½ cup ice water
1 clove garlic

Cover and blend on high speed until butter forms. This may take from 1 to 2 minutes, depending on the age of the cream. Cream that has been refrigerated for several days turns to butter faster than really fresh cream. Pour butter into a small sieve to drain. Makes 6 ounces.

Mushroom Butter

Sauté ½ pound fresh mushrooms, sliced, in ¼ cup butter for 5 minutes. Into container put

Mushrooms and pan juices

Add

½ cup (1 stick) soft butter
¼ teaspoon freshly ground pepper
¼ teaspoon salt
3 tablespoons sherry or brandy

Cover and blend on high speed for 20 seconds, or until smooth, stopping to stir down if necessary. Chill. Makes 1½ cups.

Pecan Butter

Into container put

¾ cup (3 ounces) pecan halves

Cover and blend on high speed for a few seconds, until nuts are ground. Add

½ cup coarsely cut celery
¼ teaspoon salt
⅛ teaspoon pepper
½ cup (1 stick) soft butter

Cover and blend on high speed until smooth, stopping to stir down if necessary. Makes 1¼ cups.

WALNUT BUTTER

Follow directions for Pecan Butter, using walnuts in place of pecans. Add parsley clusters in place of the celery.

Water-Cress Butter

Into container put

Leaves from ½ bunch water cress
½ cup soft butter or 3 ounces cream cheese
1 tablespoon lemon juice
Salt and pepper to taste

Cover and blend on high speed for 30 seconds, stopping to stir down if necessary. Makes ¾ cup.

Chapter 2 SOUPS

An entire book could be written on blender-made soups and soup combinations. On the other hand, half a dozen basic recipes are all that are needed to help you create literally thousands of marvelous soups for your table.

You can make wonderfully good soups from your leftover cooked meat and vegetables. For creamed soups a little cooked potato, rice, or macaroni may be used as a thickener, and no further cooking is needed. Simply heat and serve. Or serve well chilled, for there are many other cold soups, made of vegetables, stock, and cream, that are equally good or even better than the famous vichyssoise.

An electric blender brings out the flavor of soup ingredients and aerates them to an incredible lightness and consistency that cannot be achieved by any other method. It gives canned or frozen soups new palatability. If you buy an electric blender for no other reason than to make soups you will have made a sound investment in good eating!

When adding cream to a soup in the blender, add it last and turn off motor as soon as the cream is blended into the rest of the ingredients. If overblended, cream can curdle.

When chicken or beef stock is called for, it may be canned or made by dissolving a bouillon cube in 1 cup hot water.

Basic Vegetable Soup

¼ small onion
1½ cups chicken broth
½ cup cooked, leftover potatoes
1 cup cooked, leftover vegetables
¼ cup parsley clusters
½ teaspoon celery salt
1 cup cream

Into blender container put onion and ½ cup broth. Cover and blend on high speed for 5 seconds to liquefy the onion. Add remaining broth, potatoes, vegetable such as carrots, the parsley and celery salt.

Cover and turn motor on high.

With motor on, remove cover and gradually pour in cream. To serve hot, pour soup into saucepan and heat over simmering water. Delicious served chilled.

This creamy soup is equally good served hot or cold. Serves 6.

BLEND AND SERVE COLD

Avocado Soup

Into container put

- 1 large avocado, peeled, seeded, and sliced
- 1½ cups chicken broth
- 1 clove garlic
- ⅛ teaspoon hot pepper flakes or Tabasco

Cover and blend on high speed for 15 seconds. Remove cover and add

- 1½ cups cracked ice
- ½ cup cream or milk

Cover and blend for 10 seconds longer. If too thick, thin with more broth or cream and serve sprinkled with chopped chives, dill, or parsley. Serves 6.

Beet-and-Potato Soup

Into container put

1 cup sliced, cooked beets
½ small onion
1 teaspoon salt
¼ teaspoon pepper
2 tablespoons lemon juice
1 medium boiled potato or ⅔ cup mashed

Cover and turn motor on high. Remove cover and, with motor on, add

1 cup chicken broth
1 cup sour cream
1 cup cracked ice

Blend for a total of 1 minute. Serve with chopped fresh dill. Serves 6.

Borscht

Into container put

1½ cups sour cream
1 1-inch thick slice lemon, peeled
½ small onion
½ teaspoon salt
1 cup cooked, diced beets

Cover and blend on high speed for 15 seconds. Remove cover and add

1 cup crushed ice

Cover and blend for 10 seconds longer. Serve with additional sour cream for garnish. Serves 6.

Gazpacho

(Spanish Cold Soup)

Into container put

1 clove garlic
½ small onion, sliced
½ green pepper, seeded and sliced
3 ripe tomatoes, quartered

(*see over*)

AVOCADO SOUP

1 small cucumber, peeled and sliced
1 teaspoon salt
¼ teaspoon pepper
2 tablespoons olive oil
3 tablespoons wine vinegar
½ cup ice water

Cover and blend for 3 seconds, or until the last slice of cucumber is pulled down into cutting blades. Chill in refrigerator, or pour into serving dishes and serve with an ice cube in center of each serving. Serve with toasted croutons. Serves 6.

Senegalese

Into container put

1 cup (10½ ounces) cream of chicken soup
1 teaspoon curry powder
½ cup milk

Cover and blend on high speed for 15 seconds. Remove cover and add

1 cup cracked ice
½ cup cream or milk

Cover and blend for 10 seconds longer. Serve garnished with chopped chives or cucumber. Serves 4.

Vichyssoise

Into container put

½ small onion
½ cup chicken broth

Cover and blend on high speed for 6 seconds. Remove cover and add

½ teaspoon salt
⅛ teaspoon pepper
1½ cups cooked diced potatoes
1 cup chicken broth

Cover and blend for 8 seconds. Remove cover and add

1 cup cracked ice
½ cup cream or milk

Cover and blend for 10 seconds longer. Serve garnished with chopped chives. Serves 6.

BLEND, COOK, AND SERVE

Cheese Soup

Heat in saucepan 2½ cups milk, 2 tablespoons butter, and 1 clove garlic. Discard garlic. Into container put

½ pound Cheddar cheese, cubed
2 tablespoons flour
½ cup cold milk
⅛ teaspoon pepper
⅛ teaspoon nutmeg

Cover and blend on high speed for 12 seconds. Remove cover and, with motor on, gradually add the hot-milk mixture.

Pour into top of double boiler and add 1 cup chicken stock, or half stock and half white wine. Heat over simmering water. Just before serving stir in 2 egg yolks mixed with ½ cup cream and a little of the hot soup. Serve with a topping of grated Parmesan cheese. Serves 6.

Clam Consommé

(Low-Calorie)

Into container put

2 cups clam juice
1 fresh tomato, quartered
½ small onion, sliced
1 thin slice lemon
½ teaspoon celery salt
Dash pepper

Cover and blend on high speed for 20 seconds. Pour into small saucepan and simmer for 3 minutes. Serves 2. About 40 calories per serving.

Cherry Soup

Into container put all but a few whole cherries from

1 1-pound can water-pack red sour pitted cherries with the liquid
¼ cup sugar
2 teaspoons cornstarch
¼ teaspoon salt
¼ teaspoon cinnamon
2 strips orange peel (orange part only)
½ cup orange juice

Cover and blend on high speed for 20 seconds. Pour into saucepan and cook over medium heat, stirring constantly, until mixture comes to a boil. Boil, stirring, ½ minute. Remove from heat and stir in ½ cup red wine, such as Burgundy. Serve hot or chilled, garnished with whipped cream or sour cream and the reserved whole cherries. Serves 4.

Cream of Corn Soup

Into container put

1 cup whole-kernel corn
2 cups milk
1 slice bread, trimmed and torn
1 slice medium onion
1 teaspoon salt
Dash pepper

Cover and blend on high speed for 20 seconds. Pour into saucepan and heat to boiling, stirring constantly. Serves 3.

Herb Soup

Into container put

½ cup water
2 medium tomatoes, quartered
½ small onion
1 carrot, cut coarsely
1 stalk celery with leaves, cut coarsely
¼ teaspoon basil
¼ teaspoon tarragon
½ teaspoon salt
Dash pepper

Blend on high speed 30 seconds. Turn into saucepan and add 1 can (10½ ounces) beef consommé. Cover and cook over low heat 15 minutes. May also be served chilled and garnished with chopped parsley. Serves 4.

Minestrone

Into container put

½ cup water
1 clove garlic
¼ cup parsley clusters
1 medium onion, quartered
1 cup coarsely cut celery
¼ teaspoon orégano
⅛ teaspoon pepper

Cover and blend on high speed for 10 seconds. Pour into saucepan and add 1 can (10½ ounces) beef consommé. Cover and simmer 15 minutes. Into container put

2 ripe medium tomatoes, quartered

Cover and blend on high speed 5 seconds. Remove cover and add

1½ cups coarsely sliced cabbage

Cover and blend 5 seconds. Add to vegetables in saucepan the tomato mixture, 1 can (1 pound, 4 ounces) chick-peas, drained, 1 cup cooked macaroni, and 1 can (10½ ounces) beef consommé. Cover and simmer for 10 minutes. Correct seasoning with salt and pepper and serve with grated Parmesan cheese. Serves 6.

COOK, BLEND, AND SERVE

Cauliflower Soup

Simmer, covered, for 5 minutes

1 package frozen cauliflower
1 tablespoon butter
½ teaspoon salt
1 cup boiling water
⅛ teaspoon nutmeg
½ medium onion, sliced
¼ teaspoon pepper

Empty vegetables and liquid into container. Add

1 can (10¼ ounces) frozen potato soup, partially defrosted

Cover and blend. Remove cover and pour in

½ cup cream or milk

Serve chilled, or heat over simmering water. When ready to serve, divide soup into 6 small casseroles and sprinkle each serving with 1 tablespoon shredded Swiss or Gruyère cheese. Put under broiler until cheese is melted and browned.

Cream of Broccoli Soup

Simmer, covered, for 10 minutes

1 medium onion, sliced
1 medium carrot, sliced
1 small stalk celery with leaves, sliced
1 clove garlic
½ cup water

Empty vegetables and liquid into container. Add

2 cups cooked broccoli, coarsely cut
1 teaspoon salt
Pinch cayenne
½ cup cooked macaroni or other *pasta*

Cover and turn motor on high. Remove cover and, with motor on, pour in

1 cup chicken broth
½ cup cream or milk

Heat over simmering water or serve chilled with a topping of sour cream. Serves 6.

Cream of Carrot Soup

Simmer, covered, for 15 minutes 4 fresh carrots, sliced (or 1 cup), 1 medium onion, sliced, 1 stalk celery with leaves, sliced, and ½ cup chicken broth. Empty vegetable and liquid into container. Add

1 teaspoon salt
Pinch cayenne
½ cup cooked rice, *pasta,* or potato

Cover and turn motor on high. Remove cover and pour in

1 cup chicken broth
¾ cup cream or milk

Heat over simmering water or serve chilled with a garnish of diced pimiento. Serves 6.

Cream of Cucumber Soup

Simmer for 20 minutes

1 large cucumber, peeled and sliced
4 large green onions with most of the greens, coarsely cut
½ cup water
1 teaspoon salt
¼ teaspoon pepper

Empty vegetables with liquid into container and add

¾ cup mashed potato

Cover and turn motor on high. Remove cover and, with motor on, add

3 sprigs fresh mint (optional)
1 cup chicken broth
½ cup cream or milk

Heat over simmering water or serve chilled with a garnish of finely chopped cucumber and mint. Serves 6.

Cream of Lima-Bean Soup

Cook until tender 1 package (10 ounces) baby Lima beans with

2 tablespoons butter and ⅓ cup sliced scallions. Empty beans and liquid into container. Add

¼ teaspoon salt
⅛ teaspoon pepper
½ teaspoon dried marjoram
4 sprigs parsley

Cover and blend for 20 seconds. Remove cover and, with motor on, gradually add

½ cup cream or milk

Turn off motor as soon as cream is added. Pour into saucepan and add 1 can (13¾ ounces) chicken broth. Heat over simmering water or serve very cold and garnish with chopped chives or parsley. Serves 6.

CREAM OF LIMA BEAN à l'Indienne

Follow directions above, but add 1 teaspoon curry with butter and scallions to Lima beans.

Cream of Mushroom Soup

Sauté in 3 tablespoons butter until lightly browned ½ pound fresh mushrooms, sliced, 1 medium onion, sliced, and 1 stalk celery with leaves, coarsely cut. Into container put

The mushroom mixture
1 teaspoon salt
1 teaspoon Worcestershire sauce
1 tablespoon dry sherry
1 cup milk
Dash pepper

Cover and blend on high speed for 30 seconds. Remove cover and with motor on, add

½ cup heavy cream

Pour into saucepan and heat to boiling, stirring constantly. Cook over low heat for 5 minutes before serving. Serves 4.

Curried Fresh-Pea Soup

Simmer, covered, for 15 minutes

1 cup shelled fresh peas

1 medium onion, sliced
1 small carrot, sliced
1 clove garlic
1 stalk celery with leaves, sliced
1 medium potato, sliced
1 teaspoon salt
1 teaspoon curry
1 cup chicken broth

Empty vegetables and liquid into container. Cover and turn motor on high. Remove cover and add

1 cup chicken broth
1 cup cream or milk

Heat over simmering water, or serve chilled with a topping of whipped cream. Serves 4.

Potage Paysanne

Simmer for 15 minutes

2 medium potatoes, peeled and sliced
1 medium onion, sliced
¾ cup water
½ pound fresh spinach, washed
1 teaspoon chicken stock base, or 1 chicken bouillon cube
1 teaspoon salt
⅛ teaspoon pepper
⅛ teaspoon nutmeg

Empty vegetables and ½ cup liquid into container. Cover and turn motor on high. Remove cover and, with motor on, gradually pour in remaining cooking liquid. Add

1 cup cream

Serve hot, or chilled with a topping of sour cream. Serves 6.

Potage Santé

Cook, covered, for 5 minutes

1 package (10 ounces) frozen spinach
½ cup chicken broth
1 small onion, halved

(*see over*)

¼ teaspoon nutmeg
⅛ teaspoon pepper
¼ teaspoon salt

Empty vegetables and liquid into container. Add

1 can (10½ ounces) condensed cream of mushroom soup
1 tablespoon soft butter

Cover and turn motor on high. Remove cover and add

1 cup sour cream

Heat over simmering water. Best served hot. If you desire to serve it cold, omit butter. Serves 6.

Tomato-and-Dill Soup

Simmer, covered, for 15 minutes

3 large ripe tomatoes, sliced
1 medium onion, sliced
1 small clove garlic
1 teaspoon salt
¼ teaspoon pepper
2 sprigs fresh dill
1 tablespoon tomato paste
¼ cup cold water

Empty vegetables and liquid into container. Add

½ cup cooked rice, macaroni, or other *pasta*

Cover and turn motor on high. Remove cover and, with motor on, pour in

1 cup chicken broth
¾ cup cream or milk

This is best served chilled with a topping of chopped fresh tomato and dill. To serve hot, omit cream and increase amount of chicken broth to 1½ cups. Serves 6.

FROM A CAN

Baked-Bean Soup

Blend 1 cup leftover baked beans, 2 cups chicken broth, and 1 thin slice medium onion. Pour into saucepan and heat over simmering water. Garnish with strips of leftover ham or tongue. Serves 4.

Borscht

Blend a 1-pound can of beets, including liquid, 2 tablespoons lemon juice, ½ teaspoon salt, and ⅛ teaspoon pepper on low speed for 30 seconds. Remove from container and stir in 1 can (10½ ounces) beef consommé. Chill and serve with a topping of sour cream, or heat and serve with a boiled potato. Serves 4.

Cheese Soup

Blend 1 can condensed cream of celery soup, ½ cup white wine, 1 cup diced Cheddar cheese, ¼ teaspoon nutmeg, ⅛ teaspoon pepper, ⅛ teaspoon garlic powder, and 1 cup cream. Heat over simmering water. Serves 6.

Clam Bisque

Blend 2 cans (7½ ounces each) minced clams with liquid, 1 teaspoon celery salt, 4 dashes Tabasco, ¼ teaspoon dry tarragon, and 1 cup cracked ice. Remove cover and, with motor on, pour in 1 cup heavy cream. Serve with a topping of chopped fresh tarragon, chives, or parsley. Serves 4.

Crab Bisque

Blend together for 1 minute on high speed 1 can (10½ ounces) condensed tomato soup, 1 can (6½ ounces) crab meat, drained and flaked, ¼ teaspoon salt, ⅛ teaspoon pepper, 1 teaspoon lemon juice, and 1 tablespoon dry sherry. Turn into a saucepan and add 1 cup heavy cream and 1 cup milk. Heat to serving temperature, stirring occasionally. May be served chilled and garnished with chopped parsley. Serves 4.

Cream of Clam Soup

Blend 1 can (7½ ounces) minced clams and liquor with 1 cup chicken broth and ½ cup cream. Serve hot or chilled. Serves 3.

Cream of Pimiento Soup

Blend 1 can condensed cream of asparagus soup, 1 can (4 ounces) pimientos, drained, ¾ cup water, ¼ teaspoon salt, ¼ teaspoon pepper, 2 tablespoons dry sherry, and ¼ cup cream. Heat over simmering water. Serves 6.

Crème Verte

Blend 1 can condensed cream of chicken soup, 1-can measure chicken broth, ½ cup cooked broccoli, spinach or asparagus, and ½ cup cream or milk. Serve hot or chilled. Serves 4.

Cucumber-Sour-Cream Soup

Blend 1 medium cucumber, peeled and cut into chunks, 1 can condensed cream of chicken soup, ¾ cup milk, and 1 cup sour cream. Season to taste with celery salt and cayenne pepper. A dash of curry powder is excellent. Serve chilled and garnish with chopped chives. Serves 4.

Curried Shrimp Bisque

Blend 1 can frozen shrimp soup, 1-can measure milk, ¼ cup parsley clusters, and ½ teaspoon curry. Serve hot or cold. Serves 4.

Oyster Bisque

Blend 1 can concentrated cream of celery soup, 1 cup cream (or half milk and half cream), 1 can (7 ounces) frozen oysters, defrosted, ½ teaspoon dry tarragon, ½ cup clam juice, 2 tablespoons sherry, and a few drops Tabasco. Heat over simmering water. Serves 6.

Potage Nivernaise

Blend a 1-pound can sliced carrots, drained, 1½ cups chicken broth, ½ small onion, 2 teaspoons chicken-stock base (or 2 chicken bouillon cubes), ¼ teaspoon dry marjoram, ⅛ teaspoon pepper, and ½ cup cream or milk. Heat over simmering water. Serves 6.

Potage Saint-Germaine

Blend 1 can frozen potato soup, partially defrosted, 1-pound can extra-small peas, drained, ½ cup liquid from the peas, ¼ teaspoon dry marjoram. Remove cover, and, with motor on, pour in 1 cup cream. Heat over simmering water. Serves 6.

Potato Soup

Blend 1 can (10½ ounces) frozen condensed cream of potato soup, partially defrosted, 1-can measure water, 1 thin slice onion, dash pepper, and ½ cup sour cream on high speed for 30 seconds. Serve chilled with a garnish of sliced radishes and chopped green onions. Serves 3.

Russian Cabbage Soup

Into container put ½ cup water, 1 medium onion, quartered, 1 carrot, coarsely cut, 1 stalk celery, coarsely cut, ½ teaspoon salt, and ⅛ teaspoon pepper. Cover and blend on high speed for 10 seconds. Turn into a saucepan. Put into container 2 cups cabbage, sliced, and 1 can (10½ ounces) beef consommé, cover, and turn switch on high speed on and off. Turn into saucepan. Add 1 can (10½ ounces) beef consommé and 2 cups cabbage, sliced. Cover and simmer 15 minutes, or until cabbage is tender. Serves 6.

Tomato-Cucumber Soup

Blend 1 can condensed tomato soup, 1-can measure water, ½ cucumber, sliced, ¼ cup sliced green onions, 1 teaspoon salt, ⅛ teaspoon pepper. Chill. Blend in ½ cup cream or milk and garnish with chopped fresh dill or parsley.

Tomato-Sour-Cream Soup

Blend 1 can condensed tomato soup, ½ small onion, 1-can measure milk, ½ cup sour cream, 6 sprigs parsley, and a dash pepper. Serve chilled with a topping of sour cream. Serves 3.

Chapter 3 CHEESE AND EGG DISHES

There's not much of an art to beating an egg, yet the electric blender gives eggs a new almost crepelike texture—a lightness and smoothness not achieved by any other method. In addition, the blender will purée other ingredients, such as cooked ham or chicken, and cooked or raw vegetables, at the same time that it blends the eggs, bringing many a flavor change to otherwise prosaic omelets and scrambled-egg dishes.

When it comes to cheese, the blender will grate any cheese, from the soft Cheddar type to the hardest of Parmesan.

To grate dry cheese:

Grate only ½ cup at a time. Put ½ cup diced cheese in a dry container, cover, and blend on high speed for 6 seconds.

To grate soft cheese:

Again, grate no more than ½ cup diced cheese at a time. First, put into dry container 3 or 4 small chunks of soft bread. These absorb the oil from the cheese so the cheese will grate evenly and not pack together. Add the diced cheese, cover, and blend on high speed for 6 seconds.

OMELETS

Plain Omelet for One

Into container put

2 eggs
1 tablespoon water
Salt and pepper

Cover and blend on high speed for 3 seconds.

To Cook an Omelet–French Manner

In a small frying pan heat 1 tablespoon butter. When butter begins to brown, pour in egg mixture and stir rapidly with a fork until mixture begins to set. Smooth surface of egg and cook until almost set. Put 1 teaspoon butter in center and roll out on hot serving dish. Double ingredients to serve 2.

CHEESE OMELET

Blend for 3 seconds 2 tablespoons sour cream, 2 tablespoons diced Cheddar cheese, 2 eggs, and salt and pepper.

COTTAGE CHEESE OMELET

Blend for 3 seconds ¼ cup creamy-style cottage cheese, a thin slice onion, 2 eggs, and salt and pepper.

HAM OMELET

Blend for 3 seconds 2 tablespoons water, 2 tablespoons diced ham, 2 eggs, and salt and pepper.

HERB OMELET

Blend for 3 seconds 2 tablespoons milk, 2 tablespoons parsley clusters, 1 green onion, sliced, ½ teaspoon dry tarragon, 2 eggs, and salt and pepper.

MEXICAN OMELET

Blend for 3 seconds 1 strip crisp bacon, broken, 1 tablespoon chili sauce, 1 green onion, sliced, dash Tabasco, 2 eggs, and salt and pepper.

SHRIMP OMELET

Blend for 3 seconds 2 tablespoons tomato juice, 2 tablespoons diced cooked shrimp, dash Tabasco, 2 eggs, and pinch salt.

WESTERN OMELET

Blend for 3 seconds 2 tablespoons diced ham, 2 strips green pepper, 1 slice medium onion, ¼ ripe tomato, 2 eggs, and salt and pepper.

FILLED OMELETS

A filled omelet is a plain omelet which, when barely set, is spread with a meat or vegetable purée (see Index), rolled up, and turned out on a hot serving dish. It is usually served with a complementary sauce. For such sauces see Chapter 8, Savory Sauces.

Puffy Cheese Omelet

Into container put

- ⅓ cup milk
- 1 cup diced Cheddar or Swiss cheese
- 1 teaspoon salt
- ¼ teaspoon pepper
- 6 egg yolks
- ¼ cup parsley leaves

Cover and blend on high speed for 10 seconds. Fold into 6 egg whites, stiffly beaten. Pour mixture into greased skillet or omelet pan, spread evenly, and cook over low heat until puffed and lightly browned underneath. Transfer to a preheated 375° F. oven and brown top. Turn out onto heated serving plate. Serves 4.

SCRAMBLED EGGS

Plain Scrambled Eggs for Two

Into container put

- ¼ cup milk or cream
- ½ teaspoon salt
- ⅛ teaspoon pepper
- 4 eggs

Cover and blend on high speed for 3 seconds.

To Cook Scrambled Eggs

Melt 1 tablespoon butter in frying pan. When butter is hot, and before it begins to brown, add egg mixture and cook over low heat, stirring constantly, until eggs are thick and creamy. Serves 2.

Creamy Scrambled Eggs for Three

Into container put

6 eggs
½ cup light cream
1 teaspoon salt
Dash pepper
3 ounces cream cheese, quartered

Cover and blend on high speed for 6 seconds. Cook as above in 3 tablespoons hot butter. Serves 3.

MUSHROOM SCRAMBLED EGGS

Blend for 6 seconds 1 4-ounce can cooked mushrooms with liquor, 1 thin slice onion, 4 eggs, and salt and pepper. Cook as for Scrambled Eggs.

CURRIED SCRAMBLED EGGS

Add ¼ teaspoon curry powder to either of the basic recipes. Blend and cook as for scrambled eggs.

CHILI SCRAMBLED EGGS

Use tomato juice in place of the milk in recipe for Plain Scrambled Eggs for Two, and add ¼ teaspoon chili powder before blending. Blend and cook as for scrambled eggs.

CHEESE SOUFFLÉS

Cheese Soufflé I

In saucepan heat together 3 tablespoons butter and 1 cup milk. Into container put

1 thin slice white bread
½ teaspoon dry mustard
½ teaspoon salt
Pinch nutmeg

Cover and blend on high speed for 5 seconds. Remove cover and gradually add

The hot-milk mixture
1 cup diced Cheddar cheese, firmly packed

Continue blending for 10 seconds. Add

4 egg yolks

Blend for 12 seconds longer. In a 1½-quart soufflé dish beat 4 egg whites with a rotary beater until stiff, but not dry. Gradually pour cheese mixture over egg whites, folding cheese into whites with a rubber spatula until lightly blended. Bake in a 375° F. oven for 35 minutes. Serves 4.

Cheese Soufflé II

Into container put

- 1 cup diced cheese (4 ounces cheese cut into ½-inch cubes)
- 2 tablespoons butter
- 4 tablespoons flour
- ¼ teaspoon dry mustard
- ½ teaspoon salt
- 5 egg yolks
- 1 cup hot milk

Cover and blend on high speed for 15 seconds. Pour into saucepan and cook over low heat, stirring until smooth and thick. Fold in 5 stiffly beaten egg whites. Pour into a 1½-quart soufflé dish and bake in a preheated 375° F. oven for 30 minutes. Serve at once. Serves 4.

OTHER CHEESE AND EGG DISHES

Cheese Fondue

Heat without boiling 1⅓ cups dry white wine. Into container put

- ½ pound imported Gruyère cheese, diced
- 1 thin slice garlic
- 2 teaspoons cornstarch
- ¼ teaspoon freshly ground pepper

Cover and turn motor on high speed. Uncover and, with motor on, pour in

- The hot wine

With motor on, gradually drop in

- ½ pound imported Gruyère cheese, diced

Pour mixture into saucepan, and add 2 tablespoons kirsch or dry gin. Keep hot over simmering water, stirring frequently. Serve in chafing dish or casserole with chunks of French bread. Serves 4 to 6.

Cheese Rabbit

Into container put

- ⅓ cup hot milk
- 1 cup diced Cheddar cheese
- 1 tablespoon flour
- ½ teaspoon dry mustard
- ¼ teaspoon salt
- Dash pepper
- 1 tablespoon soft butter

Cover and blend on high speed for 10 seconds. Heat over simmering water and serve on hot buttered toast. Serves 2.

Buck Rabbit

Into container put

- ⅔ cup warm stale beer or ale
- 2 tablespoons flour
- 2 tablespoons soft butter
- 2 cups diced Cheddar cheese
- 1 teaspoon Worcestershire sauce
- ¼ teaspoon dry mustard
- ½ teaspoon salt
- Dash cayenne

Cover and blend on high speed for 30 seconds. Pour into a saucepan and heat over simmering water, stirring constantly, until hot and smooth. Serve on hot buttered toast and top with 4 poached eggs. Serves 4.

Cheese-and-Bacon Puffs

Brown in skillet until crisp 8 slices bacon. Make 4 sandwiches, using the bacon, 8 slices trimmed bread, and 4 slices American cheese. Cut sandwiches in half diagonally and arrange in buttered baking dish, each slightly overlapping the other. Into container put

- 3 eggs
- ½ teaspoon salt
- ⅛ teaspoon pepper
- 1 teaspoon paprika

Cover and turn motor on high. Remove cover, and, with motor on, pour in

2 cups milk

Pour egg mixture over sandwiches. Let stand 30 minutes. Bake in a preheated 350° F. oven for 20 minutes, or until puffed and golden. Serves 4.

Curried Eggs

Slice 4 hard-cooked eggs into buttered baking dish. Into container tear

1 slice bread

Cover and blend on high speed for 5 seconds. Turn out on waxed paper. Into container put

½ cup hot milk
½ cup diced Cheddar cheese
1 tablespoon flour
1 tablespoon butter
¼ teaspoon paprika
½ teaspoon curry powder
½ teaspoon salt

Cover and blend on high speed for 10 seconds. Pour over eggs in baking dish. Sprinkle with bread crumbs and dot with 1 tablespoon butter. Bake in a preheated 400° F. oven for 15 minutes, or until crumbs are browned. Serves 2.

Onion-and-Cheese Pie

Line a 9-inch pie plate with pastry. Prick pastry to prevent puffing, insert another unlined 9-inch pie plate into the pastry, and bake in a hot (400° F.) oven for 8 minutes. Remove from oven, take off top pie plate, and let pastry cool.

Sauté in 2 tablespoons butter, 2 small onions diced, until tender and golden. Sprinkle onions over bottom of pastry. Into container put

½ pound Swiss cheese, cubed
3 eggs
½ teaspoon salt
⅛ teaspoon nutmeg

Cover and blend for 5 seconds. Remove cover and, with motor on, pour in

1 cup hot cream

Pour egg and cheese mixture over onions and bake the pie in a preheated 350° F. oven for 35 minutes, or until custard is set. Serve warm. Serves 6.

Chapter 4 HOT MAIN DISHES

By preference as much as by custom, the cuisine of America is based primarily on steaks and chops. There is not much an electric blender can do to improve the flavor of a prime roast of beef, a well-cured charcoal steak, or a perfectly broiled double lamb chop. But it is in the province of sauces and gravies, in the crumbing of bread for breading veal scallops or Wiener Schnitzel, in the grating of cheese for spaghetti and casserole toppings, in the mincing of raw vegetables, the puréeing of cooked vegetables and in the judicial use of leftovers that the electric blender saves time and money and increases flavor.

And so, for many of our blender-made entree dishes, we have turned to countries whose cuisine is based on sauces, stews, and casseroles: to France, for quick variations of her renowned Boeuf Bourguignonne and Chicken Marengo; to Italy, for her *pasta* sauces and veal birds, and so on. In another chapter, on International Specialties, will be found many more interesting blender-made entree dishes to add imagination and variety to the American table.

Ham Hash

1 slice bread
2 ounces diced cheese
2 cups diced cooked ham
½ small onion
½ green pepper, cut into strips
½ cup milk
1 egg
¼ teaspoon dry mustard
2 tablespoons (¼ stick) butter

Tear bread into blender container. Cover and blend on high speed for 5 seconds.

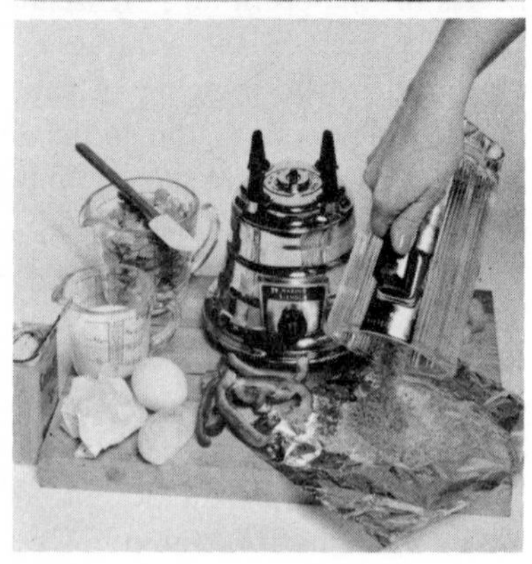

Empty bread crumbs onto piece of waxed paper or aluminum foil. Put cheese into container, cover, and blend on high speed for 5 seconds. Empty cheese on top of bread crumbs.

Put ½ cup diced ham into container, cover, and blend for 5 seconds. Empty ham into a shallow casserole. Repeat, shredding ½ cup at a time and adding meat to casserole until all ham is shredded.

Make sauce by blending onion, green pepper, milk, egg, and mustard on high speed for 6 seconds. Pour sauce over ham. Sprinkle with bread-crumb-cheese mixture, dot with butter, and bake in preheated 350° F. oven for 20 minutes.

Serve the ham hash hot, garnished with water cress. Serves 4.

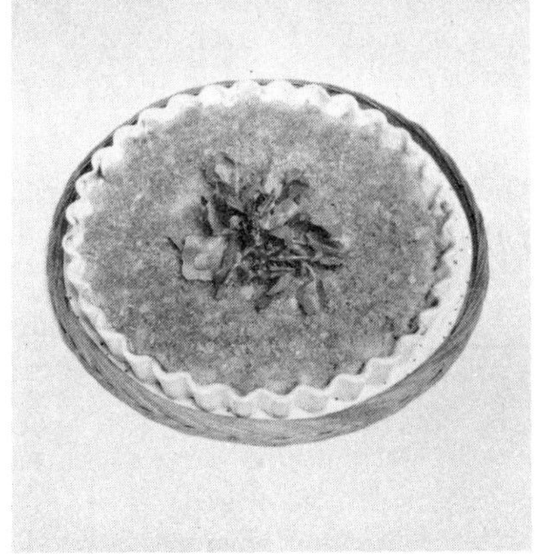

MEAT

Beef in Red Wine

Roll 4 pounds chuck or round steak, cut into large cubes, in a mixture of ½ cup flour, ½ teaspoon pepper, and 1 teaspoon salt. Reserve leftover flour mixture and brown meat over high heat in ½ cup (1 stick) butter and ¼ cup salad oil. As meat is browned, transfer to a heavy casserole. Add to casserole

½ teaspoon thyme
1 teaspoon orégano
1 bay leaf
¼ cup chopped parsley
1 teaspoon gravy seasoning
3 cups red wine
3 cups water

Into container put

1 large onion, quartered
The reserved flour mixture
2 cloves garlic

Add water just to cover vegetables, cover container, and blend on high speed for 12 seconds. Add to casserole. Into container put

2 carrots, coarsely cut
2 stalks celery with leaves, coarsely cut
The white part of 2 leeks, coarsely cut

Add water just to cover vegetables, cover container, and blend on high speed for 12 seconds. Add to casserole. Cover casserole and cook in a 325° F. oven for 2 to 3 hours. Serves 8.

Beef Roll-Ups

Drain a 4-ounce can mushrooms, reserving the liquid. Into container put

The mushrooms
¼ pound pork-sausage meat
¼ small onion
1 egg
Dash pepper
½ teaspoon salt
6 parsley clusters

Cover and blend on high speed for 30 seconds, stopping to stir down if necessary. Spread stuffing on 4 thin slices beef round (about 1 pound). Roll up and secure with string. Brown beef rolls on all sides in 2 tablespoons oil. Into container put

- The reserved mushroom liquid
- ¼ cup red wine
- 1 medium tomato, quartered
- ¾ small onion
- ½ teaspoon salt
- ½ teaspoon orégano
- Dash pepper
- 1 stalk celery, coarsely cut
- 2 tablespoons flour

Cover and blend on high speed for 30 seconds. Pour over beef, cover and simmer for 1 hour, or until beef is tender, stirring occasionally. Remove beef from sauce and cut off strings. Serve with the sauce. Serves 4.

Beef Stroganoff

Brown on both sides 1½ pounds beef tenderloin, cut into thin strips, in 3 tablespoons hot butter. Cover and cook over low heat for 30 minutes. Into container put

- 2 medium tomatoes, quartered

Cover and blend on high speed for 20 seconds. Add

- 1 4-ounce can mushrooms, drained
- ½ small onion
- 1½ teaspoons salt
- ¼ teaspoon pepper
- ½ teaspoon orégano
- 1 slice garlic
- 3 tablespoons flour

Cover and blend on high speed for 15 seconds. Add

- 1 cup sour cream

Cover and blend for 30 seconds longer, or until smooth. Pour mixture over beef and cook over low heat for 10 minutes, stirring occasionally. This dish is traditionally served with boiled potatoes, and glazed carrots and tiny onions. Sautéed mushroom caps are also good. Serves 6.

Fruit-Glazed Ham

Into container put

2 peach halves from a 1-pound, 13-ounce can peaches
3 tablespoons peach syrup
1 can (9 ounces) crushed pineapple
½ cup brown sugar
1 teaspoon ground cloves
1 teaspoon dry mustard
¼ cup melted butter

Cover container and blend on high speed for 15 seconds. Remove skin and cut off excess fat from a precooked ham. Score the fat. Cover with the glaze and bake in a 350° F. oven for 30 to 45 minutes, basting occasionally with liquid in pan. Garnish with remaining peach halves before serving.

Ham Soufflé

Into container put

4 tablespoons soft butter
4 tablespoons flour
½ teaspoon salt
5 egg yolks
1 4½-ounce can deviled ham
1 cup hot milk

Cover and blend on high speed for 30 seconds. Pour into saucepan and cook over low heat until thickened, stirring frequently. Fold in 5 egg whites, stiffly beaten. Pour into a 1½-quart soufflé dish and bake in a preheated 375° F. oven for 30 minutes. Serve at once. Serves 4.

Ham-Stuffed Peppers

Cut a thin slice from stem end of 4 green peppers. Discard seeds and white pulp. Parboil in covered pan with 1 cup water and 1 teaspoon salt for 5 minutes. Drain well. Into container tear

2 slices soft bread

Cover and blend on high speed for 6 seconds. Empty crumbs into bowl. Shred in blender, ½ cup at a time,

2 cups diced, cooked ham

Empty shredded ham into bowl with crumbs. Into container put

1 teaspoon salt
½ teaspoon dry mustard
1 small onion, halved
2 eggs
¼ cup parsley clusters
2 1-inch strips green pepper

Cover and blend on high speed for 10 seconds. Empty into bowl with meat and crumbs and mix lightly. Fill parboiled green peppers. Place in covered baking dish and bake in a preheated 350° F. oven for 40 minutes. Serve hot. Serves 4.

Lamb Curry

In a skillet melt 2 tablespoons butter or shortening. Add 1 pound boned, diced shoulder or leg of lamb. Sauté over low heat for 20 minutes, stirring occasionally. Into container put

1 cup water
1 medium onion, quartered
½ green pepper, coarsely cut
1 stick celery, coarsely cut
2 slices white bread, trimmed and torn
1 teaspoon salt
¼ teaspoon pepper
1 tablespoon curry powder

Cover and blend on high speed for 25 seconds, stopping to stir down if necessary. Pour sauce over lamb, cover, and simmer for 1 hour, stirring occasionally. Serve with cooked rice. Serves 4.

Liver Loaf

Into container tear

1½ slices bread, to make ¾ cup crumbs

Cover container and blend on high speed for 10 seconds. Empty crumbs into bowl. Into container put

1 medium onion, coarsely cut
2 large cloves garlic
½ cup parsley clusters

Add water just to cover, cover container, and blend on high speed for 4 seconds, or until vegetables are finely chopped. Drain and sauté until soft in 2 tablespoons butter or bacon drippings. Into container put

1½ pounds raw beef liver with skin and veins removed, coarsely cut
3 tablespoons flour
1½ teaspoons salt
½ teaspoon black pepper
1 teaspoon orégano
1 teaspoon sweet basil

Cover and turn motor on high speed. Remove cover and, with motor on, pour in gradually

1⅓ cups milk heated with 3 tablespoons butter

Combine bread crumbs, sautéed onion mixture and liver mixture. Pack into a 9 x 5 x 2¾-inch loaf pan. Put 2 strips bacon on top and bake in a 325° F. oven for 1½ hours. Serves 6 to 8.

Meat Loaf

Into container tear

2 slices fresh bread

Cover and blend on high speed for 6 seconds. Empty crumbs into bowl and add 2 pounds ground lean beef and ½ pound ground lean pork. Into container put

2 eggs
½ cup tomato juice
1 medium onion, quartered
1 stalk celery with leaves, coarsely cut
2 teaspoons salt
½ teaspoon pepper
1 tablespoon Worcestershire sauce

Cover and blend on high speed for 30 seconds. Add to meat and crumbs. Mix thoroughly. Pack into loaf pan and bake in a preheated 350° F. oven for 1½ hours. Serves 8.

Mock Duck

Into mixing bowl put

1 pound ground veal
1 pound ground lean pork
1 pound ground beef

Into container put

1 tablespoon salt
½ teaspoon pepper
½ cup parsley clusters
1 medium onion, sliced
2 slices fresh bread, torn
1 teaspoon thyme
½ teaspoon marjoram
½ teaspoon orégano
Dash Tabasco
2 eggs
¼ cup melted butter

Cover and blend on high speed for 10 seconds. Empty into bowl with meat and mix thoroughly. Form into an oval-shaped loaf in a shallow baking pan and bake in a 375° F. oven for 1½ hours, basting occasionally with ½ cup chicken stock or orange juice. Serves 12.

Pot Roast

Brown and cook pot roast in the usual way, but add to the pot 2 onions, quartered, 2 carrots, coarsely cut, 2 stalks celery, coarsely cut, and 1 medium potato, peeled.

When pot roast is cooked put vegetables and 2 cups pan liquid, free of fat, into container. Cover and turn motor on low speed. Switch to high and blend for 30 seconds. While blending, add 1 gingersnap or other seasoning to taste.

Barbecued Spareribs

Into container put

1 medium onion, quartered
1 clove garlic
1 bottle (12 ounces) chili sauce

(*see over*)

1 teaspoon orégano
½ teaspoon thyme
Juice from 1 lemon
¼ cup salad oil
¼ cup beer
1 teaspoon salt
1 teaspoon dry mustard
3 dashes Tabasco
1 tablespoon Worcestershire sauce
2 tablespoons brown sugar

Cover and blend on high speed for 10 seconds.

In roasting pan arrange 2 pounds spareribs, split. Roast in preheated 450° F. oven for 30 minutes, or until brown. Remove fat from pan, brush ribs generously with sauce, and continue to cook in a 350° F. oven for 1 hour, basting frequently with the sauce and turning ribs several times. Heat remaining sauce and serve with the spareribs.

Blanket of Veal

Into container put

1 cup water
1 teaspoon salt
1 medium onion, quartered
1 carrot, diced
3 sprigs parsley
¼ teaspoon ground clove
¼ teaspoon thyme
¼ teaspoon pepper
1 bay leaf
½ cup flour

Cover and blend on high speed for 15 seconds. Pour over 2 pounds diced veal and 12 small white onions. Cover and simmer for 1 hour, stirring occasionally. Add ¼ pound small button mushrooms. Cover and simmer for 30 minutes longer, stirring occasionally. In a small bowl blend a little of the hot sauce from the veal with 2 egg yolks, 2 teaspoons lemon juice, and ½ cup heavy cream. Stir mixture into the sauce remaining in the pan and cook over low heat for about 3 minutes, stirring constantly and being careful not to let the sauce boil. Serves 8.

Swiss Steak

Into container put

1 1-pound can tomatoes
1 teaspoon salt
¼ teaspoon pepper

Cover and blend on high speed for 10 seconds. Turn off motor. Add

2 large onions, quartered
¼ cup parsley sprigs
1 stalk celery with leaves, coarsely cut
1 clove garlic

Cover and blend on high speed for just 4 seconds, or until last piece of onion is drawn down into blades. Turn off motor. In large skillet heat 2 tablespoons cooking oil. In it sauté until brown on both sides 1 2-pound piece round or rump steak, cut 1½ inches thick and well pounded with 2 tablespoons flour. Pour tomato mixture over steak, cover, and simmer for 2 hours, or until meat is tender, stirring occasionally. Serves 6.

Crab-and-Macaroni Casserole

Spread 2 cups cooked macaroni in bottom of a buttered 1½-quart casserole. Into container put

1½ cups milk
1 small onion, halved
2 tablespoons parsley clusters
¼ cup flour
¼ cup melted shortening
½ teaspoon salt
½ teaspoon dry mustard
1 teaspoon paprika
Few drops Tabasco
1 6½-ounce can king-crab meat, drained and flaked

Cover and blend on high speed for 20 seconds. Pour over macaroni. Top with

½ cup blender-made bread crumbs
½ cup blender-grated cheese

Bake in a preheated 350° F. oven for 30 minutes. Serves 4.

CRAB-AND-MACARONI CASSEROLE

Crabburgers

Crumb 4 slices bread, by tearing 2 at a time into container and blending at high speed for 10 seconds. Empty into bowl. Sauté 1 medium onion, chopped, in ¼ cup butter until tender. Empty onions and butter into container and add

1 6½-ounce can king-crab meat, drained and flaked
¾ teaspoon salt
¾ teaspoon dry mustard
2 tablespoons parsley clusters
3 eggs

Cover and blend on high speed for 15 seconds. Empty into bowl with bread crumbs and mix lightly. Shape into flat cakes, roll cakes in flour, and brown on both sides in a little hot shortening. Serve with Tartar Sauce. Makes 4 large burgers.

FISH

Fillets in Herb-Wine Sauce

Arrange 1 pound (6) white-fish fillets, fresh or defrosted, in a buttered baking dish. Into container put

2 green onions or ¼ medium onion, coarsely cut
1 small clove garlic
2 tablespoons flour
1 cup dry white wine
2 tablespoons melted butter
2 tablespoons parsley clusters
½ teaspoon dry basil or tarragon
¼ cup cream

Cover and blend on high speed for 10 seconds. Pour sauce over fillets and bake in a 350° F. oven for 20 minutes, basting frequently. Serves 6.

VARIATION: If desired, fillets may be spread with bread stuffing, rolled jelly-roll fashion and secured with toothpicks. For the stuffing, combine 2 cups blender-made bread crumbs with ½ teaspoon salt, ⅛ teaspoon pepper, and ¼ teaspoon each dry basil and savory.

Fish Fillets Provençal

Defrost and separate 1 package (6) frozen fish fillets. Place each fillet on a piece of aluminum foil and pat dry with a paper towel. Into container put

2 slices medium onion
½ green pepper, seeded and sliced
1 whole ripe tomato, quartered
2 tablespoons French dressing

Cover and blend on high speed for 6 seconds. Spoon sauce over fish, dividing it among the 6 fillets. Fold aluminum foil over fish like envelopes, sealing in sauce. Place packages on baking sheet and bake in a 350° F. oven for 15 minutes. Serves 6.

Salmon Puffs

Into container tear

4 slices white bread, trimmed

Add

1 cup milk
4 eggs
¼ teaspoon salt
½ teaspoon dry mustard
1 thin slice medium onion
1 7¾-ounce can salmon, drained

Cover and blend on high speed for 20 seconds. Pour into 4 buttered individual 10-ounce casseroles and bake in a preheated 325° F. oven for 30 minutes. Serves 4.

Curried Shrimp

Into container put

½ cup water
2 tablespoons lemon juice
½ cup coarsely cut apple
1 medium onion, quartered
2 tablespoons flour
1 tablespoon curry powder

1 teaspoon salt
¼ teaspoon ginger
¼ cup orange marmalade

Cover and blend on high speed for 15 seconds. Pour into small saucepan and cook over low heat for 15 minutes, stirring occasionally. Add 1 pound shelled and deveined shrimp, ¼ cup seedless raisins, and ¼ cup blanched almonds. Cover and cook over low heat for 10 minutes, or until shrimp are cooked. Stir in ½ cup cream or milk and heat to serving temperature, stirring frequently. Serves 4.

POULTRY

Chicken-and-Mushroom Casserole

Cook 8 ounces medium noodles in 2 quarts boiling salted water for 8 minutes. Drain noodles and rinse in cold water. Into container put

2 canned pimientos
1 slice medium onion, ¼ inch thick
4 tablespoons soft butter
3 ounces cream cheese
2 tablespoons sherry (optional)
1 teaspoon salt
¼ teaspoon pepper
⅛ teaspoon nutmeg

Cover and blend on high speed for 3 seconds. Remove cover and, with motor on, pour in

½ cup hot milk

Turn off motor. Add

¼ pound (6) medium mushrooms, sliced
1 6½-ounce can chicken meat

Stir to blend, cover, and blend for 2 seconds. Stop to stir down, cover, and blend for 1 second longer. Put half the noodles into a 1½-quart casserole and add half the sauce. Cover with remaining noodles and remaining sauce. Cover with aluminum foil and bake in a preheated 350° F. oven for 30 minutes.

Country Chicken

Wipe, dry and cut into serving portions 1 3-pound frying chicken. Coat pieces of chicken in a mixture of ¼ cup flour, 1 teaspoon salt, and ¼ teaspoon pepper. Brown pieces of chicken in a skillet in 2 tablespoons butter and 2 tablespoons cooking oil. Remove chicken and add to shortening remaining in pan

1 medium onion, coarsely cut
½ green pepper, cut into strips
1 clove garlic
2 teaspoons curry powder
¼ teaspoon thyme

Cook, stirring, until onion is golden. Empty contents of skillet into container and add

1 1-pound can tomatoes with liquid, or stewed tomatoes.

Cover and blend on high speed for 10 seconds. Return chicken to skillet. Pour sauce over chicken, cover, and cook over low heat for 30 minutes. Serves 4.

Chicken Croquettes

Shred in blender, ½ cup at a time,

2 cups cooked diced chicken or turkey meat

Empty shredded chicken into mixing bowl. Into container put

¼ cup melted butter
⅔ cup flour
½ cup milk or cream
½ teaspoon salt
¼ teaspoon pepper
1 stalk celery with leaves, coarsely cut
1 small onion, halved

Cover and blend on high speed for 15 seconds. Pour into saucepan and cook, stirring constantly, until thick. Mix with meat. Cool and chill. Form into balls or cones, roll in crumbs or flour, then in egg beaten with 1 tablespoon water, and again in crumbs. Fry in hot deep fat until golden-brown. Drain on absorbent paper and serve with Mushroom Sauce. Serves 6.

Chicken Curry

In saucepan sauté in 2 tablespoons butter, 1 onion, coarsely sliced, 1 clove garlic, minced, and 2 tablespoons curry powder. When lightly browned, empty into container and add

4 tablespoons flour
1 can (1⅓ cups) beef consommé

Cover and blend on high speed for 20 seconds. Pour into saucepan and add 1 cup water. Simmer over low heat for 30 minutes, stirring occasionally. Stir in 3 cups diced cooked lamb or chicken. Heat to serving temperature and serve with toasted coconut, chutney, and chopped peanuts. Serves 6.

Delicious Chicken Loaf

Break soda crackers into container a few at a time, cover, and blend on high speed to make a total of 2 cups cracker crumbs. Turn crumbs into a mixing bowl. Into container shred, ½ cup at a time,

4 cups diced cooked chicken

Turn shredded chicken into bowl with crumbs. Into container put

½ medium onion, halved
1 canned pimiento
1 teaspoon salt
1 teaspoon chili powder
¾ cup chicken stock
½ cup milk
3 eggs
2 tablespoons melted butter
3 strips green pepper

Cover and blend on high speed for 10 seconds. Pour over chicken and crumbs and mix well. Pack into a greased loaf pan, 8½ x 4½ x 2½. Place pan in another pan containing 1 inch hot water and bake in a preheated 350° F. oven for 1 hour. Unmold and serve with creamed mushrooms or Pimiento Sauce. Serves 6.

Cream of Chicken Marengo

Remove stems from ¼ pound mushrooms. Into container put

The mushroom stems
2 medium tomatoes
¼ cup white wine
1 large onion, quartered
2 cloves garlic
¼ cup parsley clusters
½ cup flour
1½ teaspoons salt
¼ teaspoon pepper
¼ teaspoon dry tarragon
½ teaspoon rosemary

Cover and blend on high speed for 40 seconds, stopping to stir down, if necessary. In a large skillet heat 3 tablespoons butter. In it sauté 1 4½-pound chicken, cut into serving portions, over medium heat until browned on all sides. Add sauce and mushroom caps. Cover and simmer for 45 minutes, stirring occasionally. Serves 4.

Chicken Balls

Into container tear

1 slice bread

Cover and blend on high speed for 5 seconds. Empty crumbs onto waxed paper. Into container put

½ cup diced cooked chicken

Cover and blend on high speed for 6 seconds. Empty chopped chicken into a bowl and repeat, using a total of 1 cup diced cooked chicken in all. Into container put

1 egg
⅓ cup walnut meats
Dash Tabasco
¼ teaspoon onion powder
¼ cup parsley clusters
Dash pepper
½ teaspoon salt

Cover and blend on high speed for 15 seconds. Add to chicken and mix lightly. Shape into 12 balls about 1½ inches in diameter. Roll balls in the bread crumbs. In saucepan melt 3 tablespoons butter. Add chicken balls and cook over medium heat for 7 to 8 minutes, shaking pan frequently so balls are browned on all sides. Remove balls and keep warm. Into container put

2 tablespoons flour
1 cup milk
¼ cup heavy cream

Cover and blend on high speed for 10 seconds. Turn into the saucepan with the remaining fat and cook over low heat until thickened, stirring frequently. Add chicken balls, season to taste, and heat to serving temperature. Serves 3.

Chicken Velvet

In a large skillet heat 2 tablespoons cooking oil and 2 tablespoons butter. In it, sauté over medium heat until browned on all sides 1 3- to 4-pound chicken, cut into serving portions. Into container put

2 medium tomatoes, quartered

Cover and blend on high speed for 15 seconds. Add

½ cup flour
1½ teaspoons salt
1 medium onion, quartered
1 clove garlic
1 carrot, coarsely diced
6 sprigs parsley
1 bay leaf
¼ cup sherry or white wine
2 tablespoons chili sauce
¼ teaspoon pepper

Cover and blend on high speed for 30 seconds. Pour over chicken. Cover and simmer for 45 minutes, or until chicken is tender, stirring occasionally. Serves 4.

STUFFINGS

Apple-Raisin Stuffing

Crumb in blender, 2 slices at a time

8 slices bread

Empty crumbs into mixing bowl. Fill container to top with

About 2 large apples, coarsely sliced and cored. Add

Water to cover

Cover and blend on high speed for 4 seconds, or just until last slice of apple is pulled down into blades. Drain apples and add to crumbs. Add 1 cup seedless raisins, salt and pepper to taste, ½ teaspoon dry marjoram, ½ teaspoon thyme, and ½ cup melted butter. Mix lightly. Sufficient for a 5- to 6-pound bird.

Brazil-Nut Stuffing

Crumb in blender, 2 slices at a time,

16 slices bread

Empty crumbs into mixing bowl. Blender-grate, 1 cup at a time,

2 cups Brazil nuts

Empty nuts into bowl with crumbs. Into container put

¾ cup melted butter
½ cup boiling water
1 cup coarsely cut celery
2 medium onions, quartered
1 teaspoon thyme
2 teaspoons salt
½ teaspoon coarsely ground pepper

Cover and blend on high speed for 10 seconds, or until ingredients are blended to a paste. Pour over bread crumbs and toss until liquid and seasonings are mixed with crumbs. Sufficient for a 12-pound turkey.

Quick Herb Stuffing

Crumb in blender, 2 slices at a time,

1 loaf day-old bread

Empty crumbs into mixing bowl. Into container put

2 onions, quartered
¼ cup parsley clusters
½ cup (1 stick) melted butter
1 teaspoon salt
¼ teaspoon pepper
1 to 2 teaspoons mixed dry herbs

Cover and blend on high speed for 6 seconds. Mix with crumbs. Correct seasoning to taste. Sufficient for an 8-pound bird.

MEATLESS

Linguini Creole

Into container put

2 slices bread, torn into chunks
2 ounces Parmesan cheese, diced

Cover and blend on high speed for 6 seconds, or until cheese is grated. Empty onto piece of waxed paper and reserve. Cook 8-ounce *linguini* according to directions on package. Drain and rinse. Cook in saucepan, covered, for 10 to 12 minutes

1 package frozen spinach
1 medium onion, quartered
1 clove garlic
½ cup chicken stock
½ teaspoon salt

Empty contents of saucepan into container and add 2 tablespoons catchup, ½ teaspoon chili powder, ½ teaspoon salt, and ¾ cup cream. Cover and blend on high speed for 20 seconds. In a 2-quart greased casserole put a layer of *linguini* and a layer of sauce. Cover with remaining *linguini* and top with remaining sauce. Sprinkle with bread and cheese and bake in a preheated 350° F. oven for 30 minutes. Serves 4.

Macaroni-and-Cheese Custard

Cook 8 ounces elbow macaroni in boiling salted water for 12 minutes, or until tender. Drain macaroni and rinse in cool water. Into container put

4 eggs
1 cup hot milk
1 teaspoon salt
⅓ cup soft butter
¼ cup parsley clusters
1 small onion, halved
1 pimiento
⅛ teaspoon pepper
½ pound Cheddar cheese, diced

Cover and blend on high speed for 15 seconds. Mix with macaroni.

Put into greased shallow baking dish, 9 x 12 inches, set in pan containing 1 inch hot water, and bake in a preheated 350° F. oven for 40 minutes, or until custard sets. Serves 4.

Good Noodle Dish

Into container put

1½ cups hot milk
¼ cup soft butter
¼ cup flour
¼ teaspoon thyme
¼ teaspoon basil
¼ cup chopped chives or green-onion tops
⅛ teaspoon pepper
1 teaspoon salt
2 cups diced Cheddar cheese

Cover and blend on high speed for 15 seconds, stopping to stir down if necessary. In shallow buttered baking dish put 8 ounces noodles, cooked according to directions on package and drained. Pour cheese sauce over noodles and bake in a preheated 350° F. oven for 30 minutes. Serves 4.

Nutburgers

Crumb in blender, 1 slice at a time,

5 slices bread

Empty crumbs into mixing bowl. Into container put

½ cup milk
1 egg
1 slice medium onion
¼ cup parsley clusters
1 teaspoon salt
2 cups walnut or pecan halves

Cover and blend on high speed for 20 seconds, stopping to stir down if necessary. Add to crumbs and mix well. Shape into 8 medium patties. Brown in butter for about 5 minutes on each side. Serve with mushroom sauce. Serves 4.

Chapter 5 MAIN DISHES FOR HOT-WEATHER MENUS, AND MOLDED SALADS

Hot weather days pose a problem for the homemaker. Not only must meals be provided for the family, but the food put upon the summer table should be interesting, savory, and appetite-provoking. When the sweltering kitchen offers no inspiration, yet everyone must eat, the electric blender comes to the rescue.

Delicious whole meals can be prepared in an electric blender without going near your stove. The electric blender, a mechanical maid of all work, supplies the energy as you supply the ingredients for cold soups, savory mousses, tempting molded salads, chilled desserts, cole slaw, and jellied meats. The dishes in this chapter, combined with recipes from other chapters throughout the book, can be selected to make satisfying, nourishing, and palatable menus for summer dining. The following fourteen menus are only a few of the many combinations of cold dishes that can be put together into complete "stoveless" meals.

MOLDED CUCUMBER MOUSSE

Beat-the-Heat Menus

1. Vichyssoise
   Chef's Salad with Garden Dressing
   Pineapple-Cherry Divine

2. Senegalese
   Jellied Ham Loaf
   Poundcake with Raspberry Purée

3. Gazpacho
   Chicken-and-Almond Mousse
   Dóbosch Torte

4. Herbed Consommé
   Salmon Mousse
   Lemon Sherbet in Lemon Shells
   Cookies

5. Cream of Avocado Soup
   Tossed Salad with Blue-Cheese Dressing
   Strawberry Meringue

6. Clam Bisque
   Tongue-Vegetable Aspic
   Angel Food with Strawberry Sauce

7. Borscht
   Corned-Beef Timbales
   Fruited Rice

8. Tomato-Juice Cocktail
   Chicken-and-Carrot Loaf
   Mousse au Chocolat

9. Cream of Curry Soup
   Crab-Meat Salad with Sauce à la Ritz
   Pave au Chocolat

10. Fresh Strawberry-Orange Juice
    Ham Rolls on Bed of Coleslaw with Sour-Cream Dressing
    Chocolate Pie

11. Pink Clam Cocktail
    Ham Chaudfroid
    Salad with Curry Dressing
    Ice Cream with Fudge Sauce

12. Herbed Chicken Consommé
    Kidney-Bean Salad with Barbecue Sauce
    Fresh Pineapple with Minted Cream Sauce

13. Summertime Soup
    Avocado Stuffed with Crab Meat or Lobster
    Vinaigrette Dressing
    Cheesecake

14. Tomato Cocktail
    Cottage-Cheese Mold
    Pink Applesauce
    Cookies

Salmon Mousse

1 envelope plain gelatin
2 tablespoons lemon juice
1 small slice onion
½ cup boiling water
½ cup mayonnaise
1 1-pound can salmon, drained
¼ teaspoon paprika
1 teaspoon dill weed
1 cup heavy cream

Empty gelatin into container. Add lemon juice, slice of onion, and boiling water.

Cover and blend on high speed for 40 seconds.

Turn off motor. Add mayonnaise.

Add salmon, paprika, and dill weed. Cover and turn motor on high speed.

Remove cover and gradually pour in heavy cream. Blend for 30 seconds. Turn off motor immediately. If blended too long, cream might curdle.

Pour into a 4-cup ring mold and chill until firm.

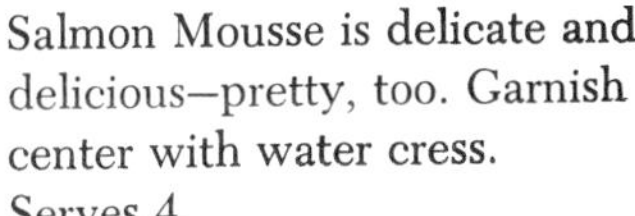

Salmon Mousse is delicate and delicious—pretty, too. Garnish center with water cress. Serves 4.

CHEESE

Blue-Cheese Mold

Into container put

2 envelopes plain gelatin
½ cup boiling water
1 teaspoon Worcestershire sauce
4 dashes Tabasco

Cover and blend on high speed for 40 seconds. Add

2 tablespoons sherry
1 cup sour cream
½ pound blue cheese, cut into chunks

Cover and blend on high speed, stopping to stir down if necessary. When smooth remove cover and, with motor on, pour in

1 cup cream

Pour into a ring mold or a 4-cup loaf pan rinsed in cold water and chill until firm. Serves 6.

Cottage-Cheese-and-Beet Ring

Into container put

1 envelope plain gelatin
1 cup hot beet juice

Cover and blend on high speed for 40 seconds. Add

1 thin slice medium onion
1 cup sliced cooked beets
½ teaspoon salt
⅛ teaspoon pepper
8 ounces cottage cheese

Cover and blend on high speed for 30 seconds. Pour into shallow pan or 4-cup ring mold and chill until firm. To serve, unmold on salad greens. Serves 6.

Cottage-Cheese Mold

Into container put

1 envelope plain gelatin

½ teaspoon salt
½ cup boiling water

Cover and blend on high speed for 40 seconds. Add

2 cups cottage cheese
1 tablespoon horse-radish

Cover and turn motor on high. Remove cover and, with motor on, pour in

½ cup cream or milk

Pour mixture into mixing bowl over 2 cups minced cucumber, ½ cup finely diced green pepper, and ¼ cup thinly sliced green onions. Mix gently. Pour into a 4-cup mold, or into individual molds, and chill until firm. Unmold on salad greens and serve with French Dressing or Cream Mayonnaise. Serves 6.

EGGS

Deviled-Egg Salad

Into container put

1 envelope plain gelatin
½ cup boiling water

Cover and blend on high speed for 40 seconds. Add

1½ teaspoons salt
2 tablespoons lemon juice
1 teaspoon Worcestershire sauce
⅛ teaspoon cayenne
¾ cup mayonnaise
1 slice medium onion
½ cup coarsely cut celery
½ cup coarsely diced green pepper
2 canned pimientos

Cover and turn motor on high. Remove cover and, with motor on, drop in, 1 at a time,

4 hard-cooked eggs

Pour into a 3-cup mold, rinsed in cold water, and chill until firm. Serves 4.

FISH

Crab-Meat Mousse

Into container put

2 envelopes plain gelatin
2 tablespoons sherry
½ cup hot chicken broth

Cover and blend on high speed for 40 seconds. Add

2 egg yolks
1 6½-ounce can crab meat, flaked
5 drops Tabasco
½ cup mayonnaise
1 stalk celery, coarsely cut
1 slice medium onion, ¼ inch thick
1 tablespoon parsley clusters
¼ teaspoon dry marjoram

Cover and blend on high speed for 10 seconds. Remove cover and, with motor on, pour in

1 cup cream or milk

Fold mixture into 2 egg whites, stiffly beaten. Pour into a 4-cup mold and chill until set, about 1 hour. Serves 6.

Salmon Pâté

Into container put

2 envelopes plain gelatin
1 cup hot chicken broth

Cover and blend on high speed for 40 seconds. Add

1 1-pound can salmon, drained
½ cup mayonnaise
2 tablespoons parsley clusters
1 tablespoon lemon juice
1 slice medium onion
¼ teaspoon salt
Dash cayenne

Cover and blend on high speed. Uncover and, with motor on, pour in

1 cup heavy cream

Pour into small crocks or custard cups lined with paper liners and chill. Remove paper liners before serving, and garnish tops with thin slices of pickles or stuffed olives. This pâté makes an attractive cold hors d'oeuvre if poured into hollowed-out lemon cups and chilled. Makes 3 dozen.

Salmon or Tuna Salad

Into container put

1 envelope plain gelatin
½ cup hot water

Cover and blend on high speed for 40 seconds. Add

¼ cup tarragon vinegar
½ teaspoon salt
1 teaspoon dry mustard
1 1-pound can salmon or tuna, drained
2 tablespoons parsley clusters
1 thin slice medium onion

Cover and turn motor on high speed for 30 seconds, stopping to stir down if necessary. Remove cover and add

½ cup chopped celery
¾ cup chopped cucumber

Pour into bowl and fold in 1 cup cream, whipped. Pour into a 1½-quart mold and chill until firm. Serves 6.

Seafood Party Salad

Into container put

1 envelope plain gelatin
½ cup boiling water

Cover and blend on high speed for 40 seconds. Add

4 tablespoons lemon juice or juice of 1 lemon
1 cup mayonnaise
½ teaspoon salt

Cover and blend on high speed for 6 seconds. Pour into a 4½-cup ring mold and chill until firm.

Into container put

1 envelope plain gelatin
½ cup boiling water

Cover and blend on high speed for 40 seconds. Add

1 cup water
2 tablespoons lemon juice
1 cup cooked crab meat, shrimp, or lobster
1 cup coarsely cut celery
1 slice medium onion
¼ cup parsley clusters
1 canned pimiento

Cover and blend on high speed for 6 seconds, or until ingredients are finely chopped. Turn into ring mold over mayonnaise layer and chill until firm. Unmold on serving platter and garnish with greens. Serves 6.

Quick-Set Salmon Mousse

Into container put

2 envelopes plain gelatin
½ cup boiling chicken broth
Juice of ½ lemon
1 thin slice small onion

Cover and blend on high speed for 40 seconds. Add

1 1-pound can salmon, including liquid

Cover and blend on high speed. Remove cover and, with motor on, pour in

1 cup cream or milk

With motor on, add

1 heaping cup crushed ice

Stir surface if necessary to help vortex pull ice down into blades. As soon as ice is mixed into the salmon mixture, pour into a 4-cup mold, rinsed in cold water, and refrigerate for 10 minutes. Unmold and serve. Serves 6.

FRUIT

Avocado Mold

Into container put

1 envelope plain gelatin
½ cup hot water

Cover and blend on high speed for 40 seconds. Add

1 tablespoon lemon juice
1 cup sour cream
½ teaspoon salt
½ teaspoon onion powder, or 1 thin slice medium onion
Dash cayenne
1 medium avocado, peeled and pitted

Cover and blend on high speed for 1 minute. Pour into a 1-pint mold, cover with aluminum foil, and chill until firm. Unmold on serving platter and serve with shrimp or crab-meat salad. Serves 4.

Cranberry Jewel Salad

Into container put

1 package raspberry-flavored gelatin
1¼ cups boiling water

Cover and blend on high speed for 20 seconds. Add

1 orange, cut into pieces and seeded

Cover and blend on high speed for 20 seconds. Remove cover and, with motor on high, gradually add

1 can whole cranberry sauce

Pour into a 1½-quart mold. Chill until firm. Serves 6.

Cranberry-Pineapple Salad

Into container put

1 package orange-flavored gelatin
½ cup boiling water
1 slice thin yellow lemon rind

Cover and blend on high speed for 20 seconds. Add

2 cups raw cranberries
1 cup pineapple juice

Cover and blend on high speed for 5 seconds, or until cranberries are coarsely cut. Pour into 6 5-ounce individual molds and chill until firm. Serves 6.

Cranberry-Relish Salad

Into container put

1 package lemon-flavored gelatin
½ cup hot water

Cover and blend on high speed for 20 seconds. Add

1 orange, cut into pieces and seeded
1½ cups cranberries, fresh or defrosted
1 cup sugar
Pinch salt

Cover and blend on high speed for 20 seconds, or until fruits are finely chopped. Add

½ cup pecans

Cover and flick motor on and off several times until pecans are coarsely chopped. Turn into a 1-quart mold or 6 individual molds and chill until firm. Serves 6.

Frosted Lime-Walnut Salad

Into container put

½ cup walnut halves

Cover and blend on high speed for 6 seconds, or until nuts are coarsely chopped. Empty into mixing bowl. Into container put

2 large stalks celery, strings removed and coarsely cut
Water to cover celery

Cover and blend on high speed for 3 to 4 seconds. Do not over-blend. Drain in sieve and empty chopped celery into mixing bowl. Add 2 tablespoons chopped pimiento. Into container put

1 package lime-flavored gelatin
1 cup boiling water

Cover and blend on high speed for 20 seconds. Uncover and, with motor on, add

1 9-ounce can crushed pineapple with juice
1 cup creamy cottage cheese

As soon as mixture is smooth, pour into bowl over nuts and celery. Mix gently and pour into an 8 x 8 x 2-inch pan, rinsed in cold water. Chill until set. Then unmold and frost with a mixture made of 1 3-ounce package soft cream cheese, 1 tablespoon mayonnaise, and 1 teaspoon lemon juice. Chill until ready to serve. Cut into squares and serve on salad greens. Serves 6.

Frozen-Fruit Salad

Into container put

1 envelope plain gelatin
2 tablespoons lemon juice
¼ cup boiling water

Cover and blend on high speed for 40 seconds. Add

½ cup mayonnaise
1 1-pound, 13-ounce can fruit cocktail, drained

Cover and blend on high speed for 30 seconds. Pour into freezing tray and freeze until mushy. Place in bowl and beat with rotary beater until smooth. Fold in 1 cup heavy cream, whipped. Return to freezing tray and freeze until firm. Cut into bars or squares to serve. Serves 8.

Golden Salad

Into container put

1 package lemon-flavored gelatin
1 cup hot pineapple juice
1 orange, peeled and quartered

Cover and blend on high speed for 20 seconds. Add

2 medium carrots, washed and coarsely cut
1 cup crushed pineapple

Cover and blend for 5 seconds only, or until carrots are finely chopped. Pour into oiled salad mold or molds and chill until firm. Serve on crisp salad greens with mayonnaise. Serves 6.

Hawaiian Salad

Mix in bowl 1 cup crushed drained pineapple, 2 chopped canned pimientos, ½ cup minced celery, and ¼ cup chopped nuts. Into container put

1 package lemon-flavored gelatin
1 envelope plain gelatin
1 tablespoon lemon juice, or juice of ½ lemon
½ cup hot pineapple juice

Cover and blend on high speed for 40 seconds. Remove cover and add

3 tablespoons salad oil
1 tablespoon lemon juice or vinegar
¼ teaspoon salt
8 ounces soft cream cheese, quartered

Cover and blend on high speed for 10 seconds. Remove cover and, with motor on, add

2 heaping cups crushed ice

Continue to blend for 15 seconds. Pour over ingredients in bowl and fold gently. Pour into a 4-cup mold, rinsed in cold water, and let set. It will be ready to unmold in a few minutes. Serves 6.

Perfection Salad

Into container put

1 package lemon-flavored gelatin
1 cup boiling water

Cover and blend on high speed for 20 seconds. Add

1 cup pineapple juice
1 tablespoon lemon juice
½ teaspoon salt
1 cup coarsely sliced raw carrots
1 cup coarsely sliced cabbage

Cover and blend on high speed for 5 seconds, or until last slice of carrot is drawn down into blades. Pour into a 4-cup mold, or into 6 individual molds, and chill until firm. Serve on crisp salad greens. Serves 6.

MEAT

Ham-and-Egg-Salad Mold

Into container put

1 envelope plain gelatin
⅛ teaspoon salt
½ cup boiling water

Cover and blend on high speed for 40 seconds. Add

3 tablespoons lemon juice
½ cup mayonnaise

Cover and turn motor on high. Remove cover and gradually add

1 cup coarsely cut celery
1¼ cups diced cooked ham
½ cup cream or milk

Pour into a 4-cup loaf pan and chill until set. Into container put

1 envelope plain gelatin
¼ teaspoon salt
⅛ teaspoon pepper
½ cup boiling tomato juice

Cover and blend on high speed for 40 seconds. Uncover and pour in

1 cup tomato juice
1 tablespoon lemon juice

With motor on, drop in, 1 at a time,

4 hard-cooked eggs

Pour into loaf pan on top of ham mixture and chill until firm. Unmold and slice. Serves 6.

Ham-and-Potato-Salad Loaf

Line a 9 x 5-inch loaf pan with foil, letting the foil extend up and over the sides. Cover bottom and sides of pan with ½ pound thinly sliced cooked ham. Into container put

1 envelope plain gelatin
½ cup boiling water

Cover and blend on high speed for 40 seconds. Add

1 cup mayonnaise
1 teaspoon salt
1 slice medium onion
¼ cup parsley clusters
1 canned pimiento
¼ teaspoon pepper
2 stalks celery, coarsely cut

Cover and blend on high speed for 20 seconds, or until vegetables are coarsely chopped. Pour mixture over 4 cups cooked, diced potatoes and 1 cup diced ham. Pack mixture into prepared loaf pan and chill until firm. Turn out on cold serving platter and garnish with salad greens and radishes. Serves 6.

Ham Chaudfroid

Into container put

1 envelope plain gelatin
⅓ cup boiling water

Cover and blend on high speed for 40 seconds. Add

1 cup mayonnaise
1 cup cream or milk

Cover and blend on high speed for 6 seconds. Spread this sauce evenly over 1 small canned ham. Chill in refrigerator for 30 minutes. Then garnish with slices of black olives and parsley clusters.

Jellied Ham Loaf

Grind in blender 1 pound cooked ham, sliced ¼ inch thick and diced, by blending ½ cup at a time on high speed for 5 seconds. Empty ground ham into a bowl. Into container put

1 envelope plain gelatin
½ cup boiling water

Cover and blend on high speed for 40 seconds. Add

Juice of ½ lemon
¼ teaspoon pepper
1 cup coarsely cut celery (2 large stalks)
½ green pepper, seeded and sliced
1 thin slice medium onion

Cover and blend for 4 seconds only. Pour mixture over ham. Add 1 cup tomato juice. Mix thoroughly. Pour into a 4-cup loaf pan and refrigerate for several hours or overnight. Unmold on bed of romaine leaves and garnish with sliced tomatoes. Serves 6.

HAM RING WITH PETITS POIS

Pour mixture into ring mold and chill until set. Unmold on bed of romaine leaves and fill center with tiny canned peas (petits pois), drained and bound with mayonnaise or with potato salad.

HAM ROLLS ON BED OF COLESLAW

Blend creamy cottage cheese with chopped chives, parsley, salt and pepper to taste, and moisten with a little sour cream. Put a good tablespoon of the mixture on each slice of ham (using 2 slices per person) and roll up, jelly-roll fashion. Chill in refrigerator. When ready to serve, arrange on bed of coleslaw and garnish with ripe tomato sections.

Coleslaw with Sour-Cream Dressing

1 small head cabbage
½ green pepper
½ medium onion
1 carrot

Quarter cabbage, remove core, and slice coarsely. Seed the green pepper and cut into strips. Slice onion and carrot coarsely. Fill container with mixed vegetables and add water just to cover. Cover container and blend on high speed for 5 seconds, or until vegetables are coarsely chopped. Drain and repeat until all vegetables are chopped. Empty drained vegetables into salad bowl. Into container put

1¼ cups blender mayonnaise
1 cup sour cream
3 tablespoons lemon juice

Stir to combine, cover container, and blend on high speed for 5 seconds. Pour dressing over vegetables, toss lightly, and season with salt and pepper to taste. Serves 6.

Corned-Beef Timbales

Into container put

1 envelope plain gelatin
⅓ cup boiling water
1 tablespoon lemon juice

Cover and blend on high speed for 40 seconds. Add

1 teaspoon dry mustard
½ very small onion
½ teaspoon dry basil
1 cup coarsely cut celery
1 cup beef consommé
¼ cup parsley clusters

Cover and turn motor on high. Remove cover and gradually add

1 can (12 ounces) corned beef, diced

Stop motor to stir down if necessary. When blended, divide mixture into 6 individual timbale molds or custard cups and chill overnight. Unmold on lettuce leaves and garnish with sliced olives and radishes. A 4-cup loaf pan may be used instead of individual molds. Serves 6.

Tongue-Vegetable Aspic

Into container put

1 envelope plain gelatin
⅓ cup boiling water

Cover and blend on high speed for 40 seconds. Remove cover and, with motor on, pour in

2 cans (10½ ounces each) beef bouillon with added gelatin

Add

⅛ teaspoon salt
⅛ teaspoon pepper

Coat bottom of a 6-cup ring mold with the aspic and chill until set. Line mold with overlapping slices of ¾ pound thinly sliced tongue or ham, dipping each slice into the aspic before putting it in place. Chill again until set. Fill mold with a mixture of 1 1-pound can tiny peas and 1 1-pound can diced carrots, drained. Pour in remaining aspic and chill for several hours, or until set. When ready to serve, unmold on serving platter and garnish center with water cress. Serves 6.

POULTRY

Chicken-and-Almond Mousse

Into container put

2 envelopes plain gelatin
½ cup boiling water
¼ teaspoon pepper
1 thin slice medium onion

Cover and blend on high speed for 40 seconds. Add

½ cup blanched almonds
2 eggs

Cover and blend on high speed for 20 seconds. Add

1 cup chicken broth
1 cup diced cooked chicken

Cover and blend on high speed. Remove cover and, with motor on, pour in

1 cup heavy cream

Pour mixture into mixing bowl over 1 can (14 ounces) tiny peas, drained. Mix gently. Pour into a 4-cup loaf pan and chill until set. Unmold and garnish with sliced cucumbers. Serves 6.

Chicken-and-Carrot Loaf Nivernaise

Into container put

1 envelope plain gelatin
⅓ cup boiling water
½ very small onion

Cover and blend on high speed for 40 seconds. Add

1 cup diced cooked chicken meat
¼ teaspoon nutmeg
¼ teaspoon pepper
½ teaspoon salt
¼ teaspoon dry tarragon
¼ teaspoon garlic powder
2 chicken bouillon cubes

CHICKEN-AND-CARROT LOAF NIVERNAISE

Cover and blend on high speed for 10 seconds. Remove cover and pour in

1 cup heavy cream

Pour chicken mixture into a 4-cup loaf pan and chill until set. Into container put

1 envelope plain gelatin
⅓ cup boiling water

Cover and blend on high speed for 40 seconds. Add

1 1-pound can sliced carrots, drained (reserve a few slices for garnish)
2 tablespoons mayonnaise
⅛ teaspoon pepper

Cover and blend on high speed for 10 seconds. Pour mixture into loaf pan over the chicken mousse and chill until set. Unmold on cold serving platter and garnish with salad greens and small cutouts of cooked sliced carrots. Serves 6.

Chicken Ring

Into container put

1 envelope plain gelatin
2 tablespoons sherry
1 teaspoon lemon juice
½ cup hot chicken broth

Cover and blend on high speed for 40 seconds. Add

¼ cup mayonnaise
2 egg yolks
¼ teaspoon dry mustard
Few drops Tabasco
6 parsley sprigs
1 slice medium onion
Dash pepper
2 cups diced cooked chicken

Cover and blend on high speed for 30 seconds, stopping to stir down if necessary. Fold in ½ cup finely chopped celery, ½ cup finely chopped green pepper, and 1 cup cooked peas. Pour into a 4-cup ring mold, rinsed in cold water, and chill until set, about 1 hour. Unmold and serve garnished with salad greens. Serves 4.

VEGETABLES

Beet Salad

Into container put

1 package lemon-flavored gelatin
1 cup hot beet juice or beet juice from 1 1-pound can and water

Cover and blend on high speed for 20 seconds. Add

¼ lemon, seeded and peeled
1 teaspoon salt
½ very small onion
1 tablespoon horse-radish
1 pound cooked beets, or 1 1-pound can beets, drained

Cover and blend on high speed for 10 seconds, or until beets are coarsely chopped. Pour into a 4-cup mold and chill until firm. Unmold on a cold serving platter and garnish with crisp greens. Serve with sour cream. Serves 6.

Green-Pea Mousse

Into container put

1 envelope plain gelatin
1 cup boiling water

Cover and blend on high speed for 40 seconds. Add

2 cups cooked peas, fresh or frozen
½ teaspoon salt
⅛ teaspoon pepper

Cover and blend on high speed for 40 seconds longer. Remove cover and, with motor on, add

1 cup sour cream

Pour into a 4-cup mold and chill until firm. Serves 6.

Green-Pea-Salmon Mousse makes a colorful buffet dish to serve 12. Quick-Set Salmon Mousse (page 86) is made twice and poured into a 3-quart mold. When set, a Green-Pea Mousse is poured on top. When unmolded the green layer is on the bottom, with the salmon on top. Garnish with lemon.

Jiffy Tomato Aspic

Into container put

2 envelopes plain gelatin
Juice of ½ lemon
1 thin slice medium onion
½ cup hot chicken broth

Cover and blend on high speed for 40 seconds. Add

4 drops Tabasco
2 tablespoons Worcestershire sauce
½ teaspoon celery salt
2 cups tomato juice
1 heaping cup crushed ice

Cover and blend for 30 seconds. Pour into a 4-cup ring mold rinsed in cold water and chill for 10 minutes. Unmold and fill center with cooked vegetables or seafood bound with Mayonnaise or one of the Mayonnaise Sauces. Serves 6.

Molded Cucumber Mousse

(Delicious Served with Cold Poached Salmon or Trout)

Into container put

2 envelopes plain gelatin
2 tablespoons lemon juice
1 thin slice medium onion
½ teaspoon salt
1/16 teaspoon cayenne
½ cup boiling water

Cover and blend on high speed for 40 seconds. Remove cover and, with motor on, add

½ cup parsley clusters
2 cups peeled, diced cucumbers

Cover and blend for 3 seconds. Chill mixture for 30 minutes; then fold in 1 cup cream, whipped. Pour into a 4-cup mold, rinsed in cold water, and chill until firm. Unmold on salad greens and garnish with sliced cucumbers. Serves 6.

SALAD DRESSINGS

If all the recipes for salad dressings were joined together, they'd reach halfway round the world! Everyone has his or her favorite recipe: some like simply a squeeze of lemon juice, a dash of fine olive oil, and a sprinkling of freshly ground pepper. Others like their dressings flavored with herbs, tomato, cheese, or sour cream. Some like them sweet, some like them sour, but most will agree that a prepared salad dressing must be well blended and perfectly emulsified.

The electric blender is the answer. It perfectly blends a simple French dressing so that the oil remains in suspension for many hours; it homogenizes other salad dressings so that they never separate, and it liquefies vegetables for refreshing low-calorie dressings. Many new and interesting varieties for all types of salads can be quickly made and blended in an electric blender. Before long the recipes will probably circumscribe the earth!

Basic French Dressing

Into container put

- ½ cup cider or wine vinegar or lemon juice
- 1½ cups salad oil
- 1 teaspoon salt
- ¼ teaspoon peppercorns
- ½ teaspoon dry mustard

Cover and turn motor on low speed. Rest hand lightly on cover, switch to high speed, and blend for 20 seconds. Pour into jar, cover, and store in refrigerator. Makes 1 pint.

Blue-Cheese Dressing

Blend 1 cup Basic French Dressing and ½ cup crumbled (¼ pound) blue cheese until smooth.

Curry Dressing

Blend 1 cup Basic French Dressing and ½ teaspoon curry powder.

Herbed Dressing

Blend 1 cup Basic French Dressing with ¼ cup parsley clusters and ½ teaspoon of your favorite dried herb—marjoram, dill, orégano, or tarragon. When fresh tarragon, dill, or sweet basil are available, use just a few sprigs or leaves.

Lorenzo Dressing

Blend 1 cup Basic French Dressing and 3 tablespoons chili sauce, 2 green onions with tops, coarsely cut, 1 canned pimiento, and several sprigs water cress, until cress is finely chopped.

Mint Dressing

Blend 1 cup Basic French Dressing and 6 sprigs fresh mint until mint is cut into fine particles.

Blue-Cheese-Mayonnaise Dressing

Into container put

1 cup salad oil
⅓ cup vinegar
2 tablespoons mayonnaise
1 teaspoon salt
½ teaspoon dry mustard
1 small clove garlic
2 ounces blue cheese

Cover and blend on high speed for 6 seconds. Makes 1½ cups.

Celery-Seed Dressing

Into container put

⅓ cup sugar
1 teaspoon salt
1 tablespoon paprika
½ teaspoon dry mustard
½ cup wine or cider vinegar
1 cup salad oil
1 thin slice medium onion
1 tablespoon celery seed

Cover and blend for 30 seconds until thick and smooth. Makes 1½ cups.

Cottage-Cheese Dressing

(Low-Calorie)

Into container put

½ cup cottage cheese
½ cup milk
1 teaspoon salt
1 teaspoon paprika
2 tablespoons lemon juice
1 slice garlic clove
½ green pepper, cut into strips
4 radishes
2 green onions, including tops, coarsely cut

Cover and blend on high speed for 10 seconds, or until vegetables are finely chopped. Makes 1½ cups.

Creamy French Dressing

Into container put

¼ cup wine vinegar
½ clove garlic
1 teaspoon dry mustard
½ teaspoon salt
½ teaspoon dried tarragon, dill, or basil
¾ cup olive oil
1 teaspoon tomato paste
2 tablespoons mayonnaise

Cover and blend on high speed for 10 seconds. Makes 1 cup.

Cream-Cheese-Currant Dressing

Into container put

½ cup currant jelly
3 ounces cream cheese
2 tablespoons lemon juice
¼ teaspoon salt

Cover and blend on high speed for 20 seconds, or until smooth. Fold in 1 cup whipped cream and 3 tablespoons chopped nuts. Makes 2 cups.

Cucumber-Sour-Cream Dressing

Into container put

- 1 cup commercial sour cream
- 1 tablespoon lemon juice
- Dash Tabasco
- ½ teaspoon salt
- 1 cup diced cucumber
- ¼ cup parsley clusters
- ½ garlic clove

Cover and blend on high speed for 15 seconds, or until smooth. Makes 2 cups.

NOTE: For Low-Calorie Dressing, make blender Sour Cream from cottage cheese, blend 1 cup cottage cheese with ¼ cup water and 1 tablespoon lemon juice for 10 seconds, or until smooth.

Gazpacho Dressing

Make blender Gazpacho, only blend for 20 seconds. Store in refrigerator. Makes 3 cups.

Fruit French Dressing

Into container put

- ⅓ cup lime or lemon juice
- 1 thin strip lime or lemon peel
- ½ teaspoon dry mustard
- ½ teaspoon salt
- 1 teaspoon paprika
- 2 tablespoons sugar
- 1 cup salad oil
- 1 thin slice garlic

Cover and blend on high speed for 15 seconds. Makes 1½ cups.

Catchup Dressing

Into container put

1 cup catchup
1 tablespoon sugar
½ cup cider or wine vinegar
1 teaspoon salt
¾ cup salad oil
¼ teaspoon pepper
1 slice garlic clove

Cover and blend on high speed for 20 seconds. Makes 2 cups.

Pimiento Dressing

Into container put

1 4-ounce can pimientos with juice
2 tablespoons blue cheese
⅓ cup salad oil
¼ cup vinegar
½ teaspoon salt
¼ teaspoon dry mustard
⅛ teaspoon pepper

Cover and blend on high speed for 10 seconds, or until smooth. Makes 1¼ cups.

Oriental Salad Dressing

Into container put

1 medium tomato, cut into sections
1 small onion, halved
¼ teaspoon curry powder
1 teaspoon dried mint, or 4 sprigs fresh mint
¾ teaspoon salt
1 teaspoon vinegar

Cover container and turn motor on high. Remove cover and, with motor on, gradually add

¼ cup olive oil

Excellent to serve on head lettuce. Makes 1¼ cups.

Sour-Cream Dressing

Into container put

6 tablespoons salad oil
2 tablespoons wine vinegar
1 teaspoon salt
Dash pepper
½ teaspoon dry mustard
1 tablespoon parsley clusters
½ small clove garlic
1 teaspoon tomato paste
¼ cup sour cream

Cover and blend on high speed for 10 seconds. Makes ¾ cup dressing, or enough for 4 cups torn salad greens or shredded cabbage.

Sour-Cream-Horse-Radish Dressing

Into container put

1 cup commercial or blender-made Low-Calorie Sour Cream
¼ cup horse-radish
½ cup chili sauce
2 tablespoons salad oil
2 tablespoons lemon juice or vinegar
2 tablespoons sugar
1 teaspoon salt
¼ teaspoon pepper

Cover and blend on high speed for 10 seconds. Makes about 2 cups.

Vinaigrette Dressing

Into container put

1 cup Basic French Dressing
6 stuffed olives
1 teaspoon capers
2 green onions with tops, coarsely cut
¼ cup parsley leaves

Cover and blend on high speed for 6 seconds, or until vegetables are coarsely cut. Makes 1 cup.

Chapter 6 INTERNATIONAL SPECIALTIES

INTERNATIONAL MENUS AND RECIPES

Americans returning from abroad have brought home with them an increased interest in the cuisine of other lands, a palate more accustomed to exotic herbs and spices, and a desire to re-create favorite foreign specialties in their own homes.

Once more, the electric blender can shorten the preparation time of many of these dishes, some of which are presented here with complete menus from a dozen countries around the globe.

The starred items in the menus are made in the electric blender.

*Coconut Punch**
*Chicken Soup with Rice**
*Pescado Caribbean**
Roast Pork
with
*Sour Orange Sauce**
*Tropical Cream**
*Sofrito**

THE CARIBBEAN

Coconut Punch

Into container put

½ cup diced fresh coconut
1 cup water
1 tablespoon sugar

Cover container and blend on high speed for 30 seconds. Strain into a bowl, pressing coconut with back of a spoon to extract all the milk. Fill wine goblets with crushed ice. Add to each glass 1½ ounces rum. Fill glasses with the coconut milk. Makes 2 drinks.

NOTE: To grate fresh coconut, put peeled, diced coconut meat into container. Cover and blend on high speed for 5 seconds. Do not grate more than ½ cup at a time.

Chicken Soup with Rice

Into container put

½ pound pumpkin or yellow turnip, peeled and coarsely cut
½ medium onion, peeled and halved
1 medium potato, peeled and coarsely sliced

Add water just to cover, cover container, and blend on high speed for 4 seconds, or until vegetables are coarsely chopped. Empty into saucepan. Add

4 cups chicken stock
2 tablespoons converted rice
1 teaspoon lime juice
Salt to taste

Cover and simmer for about 20 minutes, or until rice and vegetables are tender. Serves 6.

Pescado Caribbean

Clean and scale 1 striped bass, about 3 pounds, with head and tail. Rub fish inside and out with salt and sprinkle with juice of 1 lime. Let stand for 1 hour, then drain and stuff with the following stuffing. Into container put

⅓ cup peanuts
2 bay leaves

Cover and blend on high speed for 5 seconds, or until nuts are ground. Empty into bowl and add

2 cups blender-made bread crumbs (4 slices, blended 2 at a time)

Into container cut

1 large onion

Add water barely to cover onion, cover, and blend on high speed for 3 seconds. Drain and empty into skillet into 3 tablespoons hot butter. Sauté for about 5 minutes, or until cooked and lightly colored. Add ⅓ cup water, ¼ teaspoon salt, and ¼ teaspoon pepper. Mix with crumbs and nuts and stuff fish. Sew or skewer opening closed and place fish in a shallow greased baking pan. Into container tear

1 slice bread

Cover and blend on high speed for 5 seconds. Empty crumbs into bowl. Into container put

½ cup peanuts

Cover and blend on high speed for 5 seconds. Empty nuts into bowl. Into container put

⅔ cup cubed Cheddar cheese

Cover and blend on high speed for 5 seconds, or until cheese is grated. Empty into bowl. Into container put

½ small onion
2 tablespoons sherry
2 tablespoons melted butter
¼ teaspoon cayenne

Cover and blend on high speed for 3 seconds. Empty into bowl. Mix all ingredients to a thick paste, adding a little milk if necessary. Spread the paste over the fish, leaving head and tail uncovered. Dot with butter and bake in a preheated 375° F. oven for 45 minutes, or until fish tests done. Serve with wedges of lime. Serves 6.

Sour Orange Sauce for Roast Pork

(Aji-li-Mójili Sauce)

Into container put

4 large cloves garlic
¼ teaspoon coarsely cracked peppercorns
3 cayenne peppers

3 sweet chili peppers
½ cup olive oil
¼ cup vinegar
¼ cup lime or sour orange juice
2 teaspoons salt

Cover and blend on high speed for 20 seconds. Use as a basting sauce in roasting pork.

Tropical Cream

Into container put

1 ripe banana
2 tablespoons brown sugar
1 cup sour cream
1 can (9 ounces) pineapple

Cover and blend on high speed for 20 seconds. Serve with a topping of grated coconut. Serves 4.

Sofrito

Sofrito is a flavoring mixture for many Caribbean stews and casseroles. For generations the ingredients have been laboriously pounded to a paste in a mortar with a pestle. Today, many natives of the West Indies are making it in an electric blender. Into container put

½ green pepper, cut into strips
⅛ pound sweet chili peppers
2 medium onions, peeled and sliced
6 cloves garlic
8 leaves *cilantro,* or coriander
1 tablespoon orégano
½ cup melted lard
¼ pound diced salt pork

Cover and blend for 10 seconds. Remove cover and, with motor on, gradually add ½ pound diced cured ham to make a thick paste. Scrape mixture into a saucepan and cook over moderate heat, stirring occasionally, for 15 minutes. Cool and pour into glass jar. Cover and store in refrigerator to be used as required.

England

*Cream of Brussels Sprouts Soup**
*Roast Turkey with Stuffing**
*Giblet Gravy**
Red-Currant-and-Gooseberry Preserves
*Fruit Pudding**
*Brandy or Rum Hard Sauce**

ENGLAND

Cream of Brussels Sprouts Soup

In saucepan cook over low heat 4 slices bacon, diced, for 5 minutes, or until crisp. Add

2 10-ounce packages frozen Brussels sprouts
1 medium onion, coarsely cut
2 cups stock or bouillon
1½ teaspoons salt
¼ teaspoon pepper
¼ teaspoon thyme
¼ teaspoon basil

Cover and simmer for 20 minutes, or until sprouts are tender. Into container put half the sprouts and half the liquid. Cover and blend on high speed for 15 seconds. Pour into saucepan and repeat the blending with remaining sprouts and liquid. Pour into saucepan. Add 1 cup milk or light cream. Cook over low heat to serving temperature, stirring occasionally. Serves 8.

Turkey Stuffing

(For a 10-Pound Turkey)

Crumb 1 loaf bread by tearing 2 slices at a time into container and blending on high speed for 6 seconds. Empty into mixing bowl and continue until all bread is crumbed. Into container put

2 medium onions, quartered
½ cup parsley clusters
4 stalks celery with leaves, coarsely cut
½ cup (1 stick) melted butter or margarine
1 teaspoon salt, or salt to taste
¼ teaspoon pepper
2 teaspoons mixed herbs

Cover and blend on high speed for 6 seconds. Pour mixture over bread crumbs and mix until well combined. Blender-ground nuts or raw apples may be added if desired.

Giblet Gravy

Remove all but 4 tablespoons drippings from roasting pan. Into container put

4 tablespoons flour
1 cup water or turkey broth
½ teaspoon salt
Dash pepper

Cover and turn motor on high. Remove cover and, with motor on, add

1 cup milk
The cooked turkey gizzard and heart, coarsely cut
The turkey liver

Immediately turn off motor. Stir mixture gradually into hot pan drippings and cook, stirring in all the brown bits from bottom and sides of pan, until gravy is thickened. Makes 2½ cups.

Fruit Pudding

Crumb 6 slices bread by tearing 2 at a time into container and blending for 6 seconds. Empty crumbs into mixing bowl and continue until all bread is crumbed. Add to crumbs 1 cup currants, 1½ cups seedless raisins, 1 cup white raisins, and ½ cup chopped candied cherries. Into container put

3 eggs
⅔ cup melted shortening
½ teaspoon salt
1 carrot, coarsely cut
¼ teaspoon nutmeg
¼ teaspoon allspice
1 cup firmly packed brown sugar
½ medium orange, halved and seeded
½ cup blanched almonds
1 tablespoon brandy
1 cup flour

Cover and blend on high speed for 40 seconds, stopping to stir down if necessary. Pour over crumbs and fruit and mix well. Turn into a greased 2-quart mold, cover, and steam for 4 to 5 hours. Unmold and serve with Hard Sauce. Serves 8.

NOTE: This pudding may be made in advance. In this case, remove cover and let pudding cool. Re-cover and store in refrigerator. To reheat: steam for 1½ hours.

Brandy or Rum Hard Sauce

Into container put

2 tablespoons rum or brandy
2 tablespoons heavy cream or milk
1 cup confectioners' sugar

Cover and blend on high speed for 5 seconds. Add

½ cup (1 stick) soft butter
1 cup confectioners' sugar

Cover and blend on high speed for 30 seconds, or until smooth, stopping to stir down if necessary. Turn into serving dish and chill until firm. Makes 1 cup.

FRANCE

Onion Soup

Into container put

½ cup diced Parmesan cheese

Cover and blend on high speed for 5 seconds, or until cheese is grated. Turn out onto waxed paper. Into container put

4 large onions, quartered
2 10½-ounce cans of beef bouillon

Cover and blend on high speed for 3 seconds, or until onions are chopped. Turn into large saucepan and add 1½ cups water, 1 teaspoon salt, and ¼ teaspoon pepper. Bring to a boil and simmer for 15 minutes. Pour into a large ovenproof dish or 6 individual casseroles. Top with 2 cups cubed French bread. Sprinkle with the grated cheese and broil 4 to 5 inches from heat for 5 minutes, or until top is golden and crusty. Serves 6.

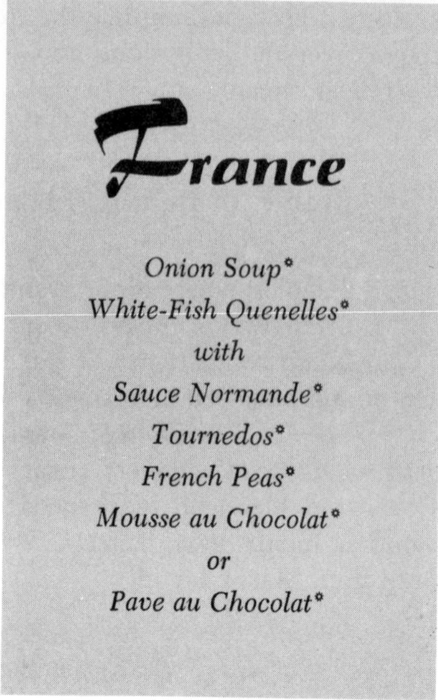

White-Fish Quenelles

Into container put

½ pound fillet of pike or other white-fleshed fish, cut into ½-inch strips
½ teaspoon salt
1 egg white
1 ice cube, cracked

Cover and blend on high speed for 10 seconds, flicking motor on and off several times. Remove cover and, with motor on, pour in gradually

1 cup heavy cream

The mixture will be smooth, thick, and creamy. Drop mixture from 2 tablespoons dipped in cold water into a large frying pan containing about 1 inch lightly salted simmering water and poach gently for 8 to 10 minutes, basting constantly with liquid in pan. Remove quenelles with a slotted spoon and place on towel to drain. If desired, garnish with poached shrimp and serve with Sauce Normande. Makes 12 quenelles, to serve 4 or 6.

Sauce Normande

In a small saucepan, heat to bubbling ½ cup (1 stick) butter, 2 tablespoons clam juice, and ¼ cup hot cream. Into container put

4 egg yolks
1 teaspoon lemon juice
¼ teaspoon salt
Pinch cayenne
1 tablespoon brandy

Cover and turn motor on high. Immediately uncover and pour in the mixture in the saucepan in a steady stream. Turn off motor. Add

2 cooked mushroom caps

Flick motor on and off twice. Set container into a saucepan containing 1 inch very hot water and let stand for 6 minutes before serving. If too thick, put container back on blender and blend for 1 second. Makes 1¼ cups.

Tournedos

Tournedos are 1-inch-thick slices of fillet of beef sautéed in hot butter for about 2 minutes on each side, or until browned and cooked to taste. They should not be overcooked.

French Peas

Into container put

4 cups coarsely cut lettuce
1 medium onion, quartered
¼ cup parsley clusters

Add water to barely cover vegetables. Cover container and blend on high speed for 2 to 3 seconds, or until vegetables are chopped. Drain. Turn vegetables into saucepan. Into container put

2 tablespoons melted butter
1 tablespoon sugar
1 tablespoon flour
2 tablespoons water
1 teaspoon salt

Cover and blend on high speed for 10 seconds. Pour over lettuce in saucepan. Add 3 cups fresh shelled peas or 2 10-ounce packages frozen peas. Bring to a boil, mix lightly, cover, and simmer for 25 minutes, or until peas are tender, stirring occasionally. Serves 6.

Mousse au Chocolat

Into container put

1 package (6 ounces) semisweet chocolate pieces
5 tablespoons boiling water or coffee

Cover and blend on high speed for 10 seconds, or until sauce is smooth. Add

4 egg yolks

2 tablespoons dark rum

Cover and blend on high speed for 5 seconds, or until smooth. Fold chocolate mixture into 4 egg whites, stiffly beaten. Spoon dessert into serving dishes and chill for 1 hour before serving. Serves 8.

Pave au Chocolat

Make Chocolate Butter Cream. Line bottom of a small spring-form pan with waxed paper. Combine 2 tablespoons cognac and ½ cup cold water. Dip 2 packages (5 ounces) ladyfingers into the liquid, 1 at a time. Arrange a layer of the moistened ladyfingers in bottom of pan and spread with half the cream. Arrange another layer of ladyfingers on the cream and top with remaining cream. Cover with ladyfingers and chill in refrigerator for 2 hours before serving. To serve: Run knife around sides of pan and invert on serving plate. Discard waxed paper and decorate with rosettes of whipped cream. Serves 8.

GERMANY

Marrow-Ball Soup

Crumb in blender, 1 slice at a time,

3 slices bread

Empty crumbs into a small bowl. Into container put

2 egg yolks
1 thin strip yellow rind of a lemon
2 tablespoons marrow
6 sprigs parsley
¼ teaspoon salt
⅛ teaspoon each nutmeg and pepper

Cover and blend on high speed for 10 seconds. Turn into bowl with crumbs and mix well. Shape into tiny balls.

In a saucepan bring to a boil 2 10½-ounce cans beef consommé and 1½ cups water. Turn heat very low. Place marrow balls gently into the consommé and let them poach in the hot soup for 2 to 3 minutes. Serves 6.

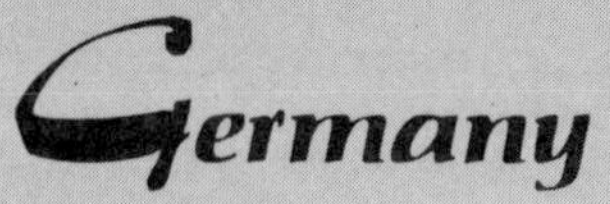

*Marrow-Ball Soup**
*Sauerbraten**
*Potato Kugel**
*Red Cabbage and Apple**
*Pecan-Nut Torte**

Sauerbraten

Rub a 4-pound pot roast with a mixture of 2 tablespoons flour, 1 teaspoon salt, and 1/8 teaspoon pepper. In heavy kettle heat 2 tablespoons fat. In it brown meat on all sides. Into container put

- 1 cup water
- 2 tablespoons brown sugar
- 2 slices lemon, peeled
- 2 medium onions, sliced

Cover and blend on high speed for 3 seconds. Pour over meat. Into container put

- 1/2 cup water
- 1/2 cup vinegar
- 3 cloves garlic
- 2 carrots, coarsely cut
- 2 stalks celery with leaves, coarsely cut
- 1 bay leaf

Cover and blend on high speed for 3 seconds. Pour over meat. Add 1/4 teaspoon cloves and 1/4 teaspoon cinnamon. Cover and cook over low heat for about 1 1/2 hours. Add 1/2 cup seedless raisins. Cover and cook for 1 1/2 hours longer, or until meat is tender. Into container put

- 1 cup sauce from the pot roast

Add

- 5 gingersnaps

Cover and blend for 10 seconds. Pour into liquid remaining in kettle and heat briefly. Serves 8.

Potato Kugel

Peel 6 medium potatoes and cube into cold water. Into container put the potatoes. Add water barely to cover. Cover and blend on high speed for 4 seconds, or until potatoes are grated. Empty into sieve to drain. Into container put

3 eggs
½ teaspoon salt
¼ teaspoon pepper
1 small onion, quartered
¾ cup flour

Cover and blend on high speed for 10 seconds, stopping to stir down if necessary. Mix with potatoes. Turn into greased casserole and bake in a preheated 375° F. oven for 40 minutes, or until brown and crisp at edges. Serves 6.

Red Cabbage and Apple

Core and coarsely cut ½ medium head red cabbage and 1 green apple. Fill container with the fruit and vegetables. Add water just to cover, cover, and blend on high speed for 3 seconds. Empty into sieve to drain and repeat until all cabbage and apple are shredded. Turn into a medium saucepan. Into container put

½ cup red wine
½ cup water
1 tablespoon apple jelly
1 bay leaf
2 tablespoons soft butter
1½ teaspoons salt
¼ teaspoon pepper
¼ teaspoon cloves
2 tablespoons flour

Cover and blend on high speed for 5 seconds. Pour over cabbage, cover, and cook over low heat for 25 minutes, or until cabbage is tender, stirring occasionally. Serves 6.

Pecan-Nut Torte

Into container put

- 4 egg yolks
- ½ cup sugar
- 6 ounces pecan meats
- Pinch salt
- 1 whole egg
- 1 teaspoon vanilla

Cover and turn motor on high speed. Uncover and stir surface of mixture with a rubber spatula, pulling mixture from sides of jar into center, until blended to a smooth paste. Stir in

- 1 teaspoon baking powder

Fold mixture into 4 egg whites, stiffly beaten. Turn batter into a 7-inch spring-form pan and bake in a preheated 300° F. oven for 1 hour, or until set in center. Remove from oven. Run spatula between edge of cake and pan, and cool. Cake will sink slightly. When cool, slice into three layers. Put slices together and frost top and sides with Chocolate Butter Cream. Decorate with whole pecans.

A HAWAIIAN FEAST

The *luau* has become popular in metropolitan cities throughout the United States. It consists of a variety of exotic Hawaiian and Polynesian dishes served in a romantic atmosphere of subdued lights, orchid leis, and soft Island music. It usually begins with subtly blended rum drinks and ends with tropical fruits and litchi nuts.

A native *luau* is a more primitive affair, a South Sea version of our American clambake, in which foods are cooked underground in a pit, or *imu*. The pit, about four feet deep, is lined with stones which are heated by means of a wood fire. The stones are covered with *ti* leaves; then the food—a suckling pig, a variety of fish, sweet potatoes, bananas—all individually wrapped in *ti* leaves—is placed on top and covered with more leaves, damp burlap sacks, and earth, and the food is "ground-roasted" for several hours. The meal is served on the ground and eaten with the fingers.

The electric blender cannot dig the pit or roast the suckling pig, but it can be a valuable assistant in blending exotic drinks, sauces, and desserts which will make a stateside *luau* an outstanding success.

The following menu is a suggestion for a modern-day *luau* which, while not typical of the Islands, reflects the tropics and is much more delicious than the traditional foods of Hawaii.

Rum Lelanie

Into container put

- 6 ounces light rum
- 1 tablespoon grenadine
- Juice of 1 lime
- 1 cup cracked ice

Cover and blend on high speed for 20 seconds. Pour into cocktail glasses and float a hibiscus blossom on top. Makes 2 drinks.

The Luau

*Rum Lelanie**
*Hilo Hattie**
*Moose Milk**
Batter-Fried Shrimp
*with Sweet-and-Sour Sauce Kaneoke**
*Barbecued Spareribs**
*Mango Maui**
Roast Suckling Pig
Roast Sweet Potatoes
Roast Whitefish
*Laulaus with Curry Sauce**
*Coconut Cream**
*Papaya Pali**

Hilo Hattie

Into container put

1 cup cracked ice
1 tablespoon lime juice
3 ounces light rum
¾ ounces Cointreau or Triple Sec
1 drop green food coloring

Cover container and blend on high speed for 20 seconds. Pour into champagne glasses and decorate with small gardenias. Makes 2 drinks.

Moose Milk

Into container put

¼ cup vodka
1 egg
½ cup sugar
1 tablespoon orange-flower water*
¼ cup lemon juice
6 ice cubes, cracked

Cover container and blend on high speed for 10 seconds. Remove cover and, with motor on, add

About 2 cups milk, or enough to fill container

Pour into goblets. Makes 4 drinks.

Sweet-and-Sour Sauce Kaneoke

Into container put

1 cup canned crushed pineapple with juice
1 tablespoon soy sauce
1 teaspoon curry powder
¼ teaspoon salt
1 teaspoon tomato paste

Cover and blend on high speed for 20 seconds, or until smooth. Serve as a sauce with batter-fried shrimp.

NOTE: For batter for fried shrimp, see Index.

* This may be purchased in drugstore.

Barbecued Spareribs

Into container put

1 medium onion, quartered
1 clove garlic
1 bottle (12 ounces) chili sauce
Juice of 1 lemon
¼ cup salad oil
1 teaspoon salt
1 teaspoon dry mustard
1 teaspoon chili powder
½ teaspoon pepper
½ teaspoon paprika
3 dashes Tabasco
2 tablespoons Worcestershire sauce
3 tablespoons honey
1 tablespoon vinegar
½ cup beer

Cover container and blend on high speed for 20 seconds. Pour into saucepan and bring to a boil. Spread spareribs, cut into small pieces, in roasting pan and brush generously with the sauce. Bake in a 350° F. oven for 1 hour, basting frequently with the sauce and turning the ribs several times. Simmer remaining sauce for 1 hour and serve with the spareribs.

Mango Maui

Into container put

½ cup canned crushed pineapple
¼ cup pineapple juice from can
8 ounces soft cream cheese
2 tablespoons syrup from jar of chutney
¼ teaspoon garlic powder
¼ teaspoon ginger
1 tablespoon peach brandy (optional)

Cover container and turn blender on high. Remove cover and stir surface of mixture with rubber spatula, being careful not to dip too deeply into mixture, until thoroughly blended. Pour into a bowl set in center of a platter and sprinkle with blender-chopped *macadamia* nuts. Surround by small wooden sticks on which are strung small balls of mango, papaya, or other melon.

LAULAUS WITH CURRY SAUCE

Remove meat from a plump roasting chicken and cut it into squares. Place several large spinach leaves crosswise on table and put a piece each of white and dark meat on the leaves. Sprinkle with salt and pepper and a little finely chopped onion and fold spinach leaves over filling. Wrap each package in *ti* leaves or aluminum foil and tie with string. Cook in pit with other foods or steam in a covered steamer for about 2½ hours. Serve with Curry Sauce.

Curry Sauce

Into container put

2 cups hot milk
1 cup diced fresh coconut

Cover and blend on high speed for 30 seconds. Strain into a bowl, pressing coconut with back of a wooden spoon to extract all the milk. Into container put

2 tablespoons butter
½ medium onion, sliced
1 clove garlic
1 piece candied ginger
1 tablespoon curry powder
1 tablespoon brown sugar
1 slice canned pineapple, or 6 chunks
2 tablespoons pineapple juice
2 slices bread with crusts, broken
¼ teaspoon salt, or salt to taste
½ cup of the coconut milk

Cover and turn motor on high speed. Uncover and, with motor on, gradually add remaining coconut milk. Pour sauce into saucepan and cook over simmering water for 30 minutes, stirring occasionally. Makes 1 pint.

Coconut Cream

Into container put

½ cup hot coconut milk
2 envelopes plain gelatin

Cover and blend on high speed for 40 seconds. Add

3 egg yolks
⅓ cup sugar
2 teaspoons vanilla

Cover container and turn motor on high. Uncover and pour in

1 cup cold coconut milk
½ cup cream
Enough crushed ice to bring liquid to top of container

Pour into a 4-cup mold and refrigerate for 10 minutes. Serves 6.

NOTE: For frozen coconut cream pour into ice-cube tray and freeze until solid. Unmold and cut into squares. Garnish with grated fresh coconut and sprinkle with rum.

Papaya Pali

If papaya are not available, use a fine ripe cantaloupe. Into container put

Juice of ½ lemon
2 envelopes gelatin
½ cup hot papaya juice or apricot nectar

Cover and blend on high speed for 40 seconds. Add

⅓ cup sugar

Cover and blend for 3 seconds. Remove cover and, with motor on, add

1 cup diced papaya or cantaloupe
1 cup cream
Enough crushed ice to bring liquid to top of container

Turn off motor, let the *pali* set for 1 minute, then spoon into serving glasses. If desired, top with a spoonful of rum. Serves 6.

INDIA

Mint Soup

Into container put

1½ cups water
2 cloves garlic
2 tablespoons fresh mint, or 2 teaspoons dried mint
⅛ teaspoon chili powder
2 tablespoons flour
1 teaspoon salt

Cover and blend on high speed for 10 seconds. Turn into saucepan and add 2 10½-ounce cans beef consommé. Bring to a boil and simmer for 10 minutes, stirring occasionally. Pour into soup tureen containing 3 lightly beaten eggs. Serves 4.

Indian Curry Sauce

(For Fish, Meat, or Eggs)

Into container put

2 medium onions, halved
1 apple, cored and quartered
2 cloves garlic

Add water barely to cover, cover, and blend on high speed for 3 or 4 seconds, or until vegetables are finely chopped. Turn into saucepan. Into container put

½ cup preserved watermelon rind
⅓ cup water
2 tablespoons lemon juice
1 teaspoon turmeric
1 teaspoon coriander
1 teaspoon cumin
½ teaspoon pepper
½ teaspoon ginger
¼ teaspoon cayenne
¼ teaspoon mace
¼ teaspoon cardamom

⅛ teaspoon dry mustard
⅛ teaspoon cloves
⅛ teaspoon poppy seeds
1 bay leaf
½ cinnamon stick

Cover and blend on high speed for 15 seconds. Add to vegetables and liquid in saucepan and bring to a boil. Cover and simmer for 1¼ hours or until thickened, stirring occasionally. Return to container and blend on high speed for 15 seconds, or until smooth: put into container about 1 cup sauce. Cover, turn motor on high, remove cover, and gradually pour in rest of sauce. Return to saucepan. Add 2 cups cooked fish, meat, or hard-cooked eggs (about 8), and heat to serving temperature over simmering water. Serves 4.

Raw-Apple Chutney

Core and coarsely cut 2 apples. Seed 1 medium green pepper and cut into strips. Peel 1 clove garlic. Fill container with the prepared ingredients. Add water barely to cover, cover, and blend on high speed for 2 to 3 seconds, or until vegetables are chopped. Drain and turn into a mixing bowl. Repeat, using remaining vegetables. To chopped vegetables add

1 tablespoon vinegar
1 tablespoon lemon juice
¼ teaspoon salt
¼ teaspoon ginger
¼ teaspoon cayenne
¾ teaspoon paprika
½ cup seedless raisins

Mix and chill. Makes about 2½ cups.

*Mint Soup**
*Indian Curry Sauce**
*Raw-Apple Chutney**
*Cucumbers with Turmeric**
*Eggplant Salad**
*Pineapple Rose Crush**

Cucumbers with Turmeric

Into container put

3 cloves garlic
2 scallions or green onions, coarsely cut
1½ teaspoons turmeric
1 teaspoon ginger
1 teaspoon salt
⅓ cup water
¼ cup vinegar
¼ cup sugar

Cover and blend on high speed for 10 seconds. Turn into small saucepan and simmer for 15 minutes. Pour over 4 cucumbers, peeled, seeded, and cut into 2-inch strips. Chill for 2 to 3 hours, stirring occasionally. Serves 6.

Eggplant Salad

Cut a medium eggplant in half and place it cut side down on a greased baking sheet. Bake in a preheated 350° F. oven for 40 minutes. Cool and scoop out pulp. Into container put

About ¼ of the eggplant
¼ cup lemon juice
2 tablespoons olive or sesame-seed oil
¾ teaspoon salt
1 teaspoon sesame seeds
Dash Tabasco

Cover and blend on high speed for 15 seconds. Remove cover and gradually add remaining eggplant, stopping to stir down if necessary. Spoon into 6 lettuce cups and sprinkle with paprika. Chill. Serves 6.

Pineapple Rose Crush

Into container put

Petals from 6 pungent roses, reserving 6 petals for garnish
½ cup water

Cover and blend on high speed for 20 seconds. Let stand, covered, for 1 hour. Strain the rose water through sieve lined with cheesecloth and set aside. Peel, core, and coarsely cut a medium pineapple. Into container put

- The rose water
- 2 tablespoons lemon juice
- About ½ cup pineapple chunks

Cover and blend on high speed for 3 to 4 seconds. Remove cover and, with motor on, gradually add remaining pineapple. Turn into 6 sherbet glasses and sprinkle with sugar. Top each with a rose petal and chill. Serves 6.

ITALY

FRITTO MISTO

Fritto Misto, or mixed fry, consists of all manner of vegetables—such as asparagus, zucchini or eggplant slices, onion rings, cooked broccoli, carrots or cauliflower flowerets—shrimp, slices of white-meat fish, poached sweetbreads, etc. dipped in batter and fried until lightly browned in deep shortening heated to 365° F. Drain, sprinkle with salt, and serve with wedges of lemon or lime.

Frying Batter

Into container put

- 1 cup beer or milk
- 1 teaspoon salt
- 2 eggs
- 2 tablespoons oil
- ⅛ teaspoon cayenne
- 1¼ cups all-purpose flour

Cover and blend on high speed for 10 seconds, or until flour is blended. Let stand for 5 minutes. Makes 1½ cups batter, or enough for a serving of batter-fried foods for 6.

*Fritto Misto**
*Chicken Lasagne**
or
*Baked Manicotti with Tomato Sauce**
*Stuffed Veal Birds**
Rice
*Squash with Peppers**
*Eggplant Sicilienne**
*Biscuit Tortoni**

Chicken Lasagne

Into container put

- 1 cup diced cooked chicken
- 1 small onion, quartered
- 1 clove garlic
- 6 sprigs parsley
- 1 6-ounce can tomato paste
- ¾ cup water
- ½ teaspoon salt
- ¼ teaspoon pepper
- 1 teaspoon sugar

Cover and blend on high speed for 40 seconds, stopping to stir down if necessary. In a shallow greased baking dish arrange alternate layers of the sauce, ½ pound lasagne, cooked and drained, and 2 cups *ricotta* or cottage cheese. Cover top with ½ pound *mozzarella* cheese, thinly sliced. Sprinkle with ¼ cup grated Parmesan cheese. Bake in a preheated 350° F. oven for 25 minutes. Serves 4 to 6.

Baked Manicotti with Tomato Sauce

Into container put

- 2 cloves garlic
- 1 medium onion, sliced
- ¼ teaspoon basil
- ¼ teaspoon celery salt
- ¼ teaspoon orégano
- 1 tablespoon parsley clusters
- ½ teaspoon salt
- ½ cup white wine or sauterne
- ½ pound mushrooms, halved

Cover and blend on high speed for 15 seconds. Add

- 1 6-ounce can tomato paste
- 1 can (1 pound) tomatoes
- 5 olives, pitted and sliced
- 1 tablespoon capers

Cover and blend on low speed for 15 seconds. Fill cooked *manicotti* or large shell macaroni with *ricotta* cheese. Arrange the stuffed *pasta* in a buttered casserole. Pour over the sauce and bake in a preheated 350° F. oven for 20 minutes.

Stuffed Veal Birds

Into container tear

- 2 slices bread

Cover and blend on high speed for 10 seconds. Empty crumbs into bowl and repeat twice more, using a total of 6 slices bread to make 3 cups crumbs. Into container put

- ¼ cup hot water
- 1 medium onion, coarsely sliced
- 1 teaspoon salt
- ¼ teaspoon pepper
- ¼ cup melted butter
- 2 tablespoons parsley clusters
- ½ cup coarsely cut celery
- ¾ teaspoon sage

Cover and blend on high speed for 10 seconds. Empty into crumbs and mix well. Place dressing on 1½ pounds veal, cut into 6 serving pieces and thinly pounded. Roll up veal and tie with string. Dredge meat with flour and brown in butter or drippings. Transfer to baking dish and add stock or bouillon to cover and ½ cup cream. Cover and bake in a 325° F. oven for 1½ hours. Gravy may be thickened if desired by stirring in 1 tablespoon flour mixed to a paste with 1 tablespoon soft butter. Serves 6.

Squash with Peppers

Coarsely slice 4 summer squash. Seed 3 green peppers and cut into strips. Fill container loosely with the prepared ingredients and add water barely to cover. Cover and blend on high speed for 3 to 4 seconds, or until vegetables are coarsely chopped. Drain and set aside. Repeat until all vegetables have been chopped and drained. In saucepan heat ½ cup salad oil. Add the drained vegetables and sauté for 10 minutes. Into container put

1 tomato, quartered
1½ teaspoons salt
⅛ teaspoon pepper
1 teaspoon sugar
½ teaspoon dry basil

Cover and blend on high speed for 10 seconds. Pour tomato mixture over vegetables, cover, and simmer for 10 minutes. Serves 6.

Eggplant Sicilienne

Into container tear

2 slices bread

Cover and blend on high speed for 10 seconds. Empty crumbs onto waxed paper. Into container put

½ cup cubed Cheddar cheese

Cover and blend on high speed for 6 seconds. Empty grated cheese onto paper and mix with crumbs. Into container put

1 1-pound, 4-ounce can tomatoes
1 medium onion, sliced
2 large cloves garlic
1 teaspoon salt
1 teaspoon orégano

½ teaspoon thyme
½ teaspoon basil
¼ teaspoon pepper

Cover and blend on high speed for 5 seconds. Remove cover, and with motor on, slice into container

2 stalks celery
2 carrots

Turn off motor and pour mixture into large saucepan. Pare, and cut into 1-inch cubes 1 medium eggplant. Add to saucepan and mix. Cover and cook over low heat for 30 minutes. Transfer to casserole and top with cheese and crumbs. Bake in a preheated 375° F. oven for 20 minutes, or until browned and bubbly. Serves 6.

Biscuit Tortoni

Into container put

⅓ cup toasted blanched almonds

Cover and blend on high speed for 5 seconds, or until nuts are ground. Turn out onto waxed paper. In small saucepan combine 2 tablespoons water and ⅓ cup sugar. Bring to a boil and boil for 3 minutes. Into container put

2 tablespoons sherry
3 egg yolks

Cover container and turn motor on high. Remove cover and, with motor on, gradually pour in the hot syrup in a steady stream. Turn off motor. Fold yolk mixture into 1 cup heavy cream, whipped. Arrange 8 individual paper soufflé cups in a refrigerator tray. Pour cream into the cups, sprinkle with the ground nuts and freeze for 2 to 3 hours. Serves 8.

MEXICO

Guacamole

Into container put

1 ripe avocado, peeled, seeded, and sliced
1 clove garlic
½ teaspoon hot red-pepper flakes
3 tablespoons lemon or lime juice, or juice of 1 lemon or lime
4 tablespoons olive oil
¼ teaspoon salt

Cover and turn motor on high. Remove cover and stir surface of mixture with a rubber spatula, being careful not to dip deeply, until thoroughly blended. Serve as a dip for raw vegetables or on sesame-seed crackers. Makes about 1 cup.

Scrambled Eggs and Peppers Mexicana

Into container put

½ medium onion, coarsely cut
1 clove garlic
2 green peppers, seeded and cut into strips

*Guacamole**
*Scrambled Eggs and Peppers Mexicana**
*Chili con Carne**
with
*Green Sauce**
or
*Chicken Mole**
*Mango Cream**

½ cup tomato purée
1 teaspoon salt
¼ teaspoon pepper
6 eggs

Cover and blend on high speed for 3 seconds. In a skillet heat 3 tablespoons butter. Add the eggs and stir over low heat until eggs are the consistency of heavy cream. Serve on toast or *tortillas.* Serves 3.

Chili Con Carne

Cook 2 pounds cubed beef in simmering salted water to cover for 30 minutes. Into container put

6 chili peppers*
2 cloves garlic
1 teaspoon dry orégano
1 cup beef bouillon
½ cup water
2 tablespoons flour
¼ cup olive oil
⅛ teaspoon cumin

Cover and blend on high speed for 10 seconds, or until smooth. Add sauce to meat, stir to blend, and continue to cook, covered, for about 1 hour longer, or until meat is tender. Serve with Mexican beans. Serves 6.

Green Sauce

Into container put

2 large green peppers, seeded and cut into strips
1 tomato, quartered
1 large onion, sliced
1 clove garlic
½ cucumber, peeled and sliced
¼ cup each vinegar and water
½ cup olive oil

(*see over*)

* If chili peppers are dry they should be soaked in warm water for about 20 minutes to soften, then drained and seeded.

1 tablespoon sugar
¼ teaspoon cinnamon
¼ teaspoon cloves
1 teaspoon salt

Cover and blend on high speed for 12 seconds. Pour into saucepan and simmer for 15 minutes, or until thick. Serve with meat or eggs.

Chicken Mole

Simmer 1 4-pound chicken, cut into serving pieces, in salted water to cover until tender. Drain, reserving broth, and brown pieces in a large kettle in 2 tablespoons salad oil. Into container put

1 ounce (1 square) unsweetened chocolate, cut into pieces

Cover and blend on high speed for 10 seconds. Empty onto waxed paper and set aside. Into container put

1 green pepper, seeded and cut into strips
1 red pepper, seeded and cut into strips

Add water just to cover, cover container, and blend on high speed for 5 to 6 seconds, or until vegetables are finely chopped. Drain and add to the chicken. Into container put

2 cups chicken broth
1 medium onion, coarsely cut
½ teaspoon dried hot peppers
1 large clove garlic
3 peppercorns
¼ teaspoon coriander seeds
¼ teaspoon anise seeds
1 teaspoon sesame seeds
3 tablespoons tomato paste
2 tablespoons brown sugar
1 teaspoon salt
The grated chocolate

Cover and blend on low speed for 30 seconds. Switch to high and blend for 10 seconds longer. Pour over chicken and peppers. Cover kettle, bring liquid to a boil, and simmer for 30 minutes. Serve with cooked rice and fried bananas. Serves 4.

NOTE: This is a fairly hot sauce. For a milder flavor, reduce quantity of hot peppers.

Mango Cream

Into container put

2 mangoes,* peeled and the pulp cut away from the pits
Juice of 1 large orange
½ cup confectioners' sugar

Cover container and blend on high speed for 10 seconds, or until fruit is reduced to a smooth purée. Empty into bowl and fold in 1 cup heavy cream, whipped, and ⅓ cup coarsely chopped pecans. Spoon into sherbet glasses and refrigerate until chilled. Serves 6.

THE NEAR EAST

Taheeni

(A Favorite Cocktail Dip in Lebanon)

Cut a thin slice from bottom and top of 1 medium eggplant and bake in a 350° F. oven for about 1½ hours, or until tender. Split and remove pulp. Into container put

1 cup eggplant pulp
3 tablespoons lemon juice
3 tablespoons olive or sesame oil
1 clove garlic
1 teaspoon salt

Cover and blend on high speed for 1 minute, or until very smooth and creamy. Pour into a bowl and fold in 1 tablespoon sesame seeds and 1 tablespoon chopped parsley. Serve with vegetable sticks or crackers. Makes about 1½ cups.

Stuffed Lettuce or Vine Leaves

In a large skillet heat 1 tablespoon oil. Add ½ cup rice and ⅓ cup pine nuts. Cook over low heat for 10 minutes. Into container put

1 slice garlic
½ small onion

(*see over*)

* Mangoes can be bought in specialty food markets and metropolitan fruit stores during the fall months.

¼ cup parsley clusters
¼ teaspoon pepper
¼ teaspoon dill weed
¼ teaspoon thyme
1½ teaspoons salt
1 teaspoon paprika
1 tablespoon lemon juice
1 egg
1 thin strip yellow rind of a lemon
⅛ teaspoon nutmeg

Cover and blend on high speed for 10 seconds. Pour over rice and mix. Pour boiling water over 12 large lettuce or vine leaves and let stand 3 minutes. Drain. Spoon about 1 tablespoon rice mixture into center of each leaf. Roll up leaf from stem end halfway. Fold in either side to make a packet and continue rolling to seal. Place rolls in a skillet and add 1¼ cups water. Top with a plate or layer-cake pan to prevent rolls from opening. Simmer for 30 minutes. Leave rolls in skillet. Sprinkle with 1 tablespoon lemon juice and 2 tablespoons salad or olive oil. Chill and serve with lemon wedges. Makes 12 hors d'oeuvre.

Lentil Soup

Into large saucepan put

1 pound (2 cups) lentils
6 cups water
1½ teaspoons salt
½ teaspoon pepper
2 medium onions

Bring to a boil, cover, and simmer for 40 minutes. Fill container half full of soup. Cover and blend on high speed for 10 seconds, or until smooth. Pour into saucepan. Repeat until all soup has been blended. Into container put

4 cups spinach
2 tablespoons lemon juice
¼ teaspoon Tabasco

Add water just to cover. Cover and blend on high speed for 2 to 3 seconds, or until spinach is finely chopped. Add to soup. Bring to a boil and simmer for 10 minutes. Serves 8.

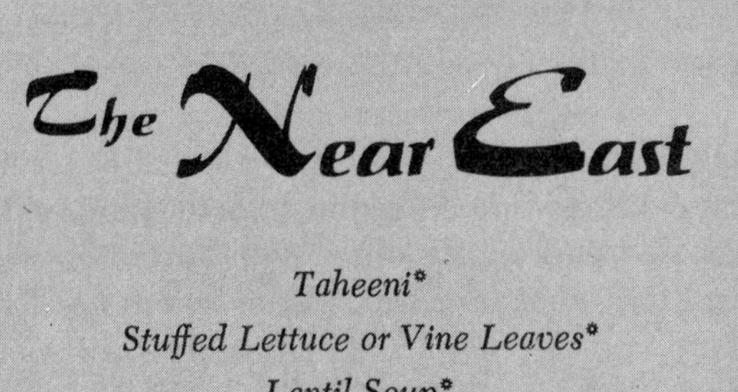

*Taheeni**
*Stuffed Lettuce or Vine Leaves**
*Lentil Soup**
*Circassian Chicken**
or
*Baked Lamb**
*Leeks and Olives**
*Tabbouleh**
*Salatit Khyaar bi Laban**
*Orange Custard Pudding**

Circassian Chicken

In large saucepan put

- 3 quarts water
- 1 medium onion
- 1 carrot
- 1 stalk celery with leaves
- ½ cup parsley clusters
- 1 teaspoon salt
- ½ teaspoon pepper
- 1 4-pound chicken

Bring to a boil, cover, and simmer for 1½ hours, or until chicken is tender. Remove 1 cup cooking liquid. Cool chicken in remaining liquid. Into container tear 3 slices bread. Add 1 cup cooking liquid, cover, and turn motor on high. Gradually add 2 cups walnut meats. Blend to a smooth paste, stopping to stir down if necessary. Slice chicken and spread with the walnut paste. Arrange on serving platter and sprinkle with paprika. Garnish with parsley and chill. Serves 6.

Baked Lamb

Into container put

1½ cups cracked wheat

Cover and blend on high speed for 25 seconds, or until wheat is ground. Empty into large bowl. Into container put 2 medium onions, quartered, and add water just to cover. Cover and blend on high speed for 3 or 4 seconds, or until onions are finely chopped. Drain. Return half the chopped onions to the container and add

1 egg
½ teaspoon dry basil
1½ teaspoons salt
¼ teaspoon pepper

Cover and blend on high speed for 10 seconds. Pour into bowl with wheat. Add 1 pound lean ground lamb. Mix well and spread half the mixture in bottom of a greased 9-inch square pan. Mix together in a bowl the remaining chopped onion, 1 pound lean ground lamb, ½ cup pine nuts, and 1 teaspoon salt. Spread over wheat mixture in pan. Top with remaining wheat mixture and spread with knife to get a flat surface. Run knife around edges of pan and cut meat into 6 pieces. Bake in a preheated 375° F. oven for 1 hour. Serve hot. Serves 6.

Leeks and Olives

Thoroughly wash and coarsely cut 1 pound leeks. Fill container with the leeks. Add water just to cover. Cover and blend on high speed for 3 to 4 seconds, or until leeks are coarsely chopped. Drain, reserving 1½ cups water. Empty chopped leeks into saucepan. Repeat until all leeks have been chopped. Into container put

1½ cups reserved water
1 tablespoon salad oil
3 tablespoons tomato paste
2 tablespoons flour
2 teaspoons salt
¼ teaspoon pepper
2 tablespoons lemon juice

Cover and blend on high speed for 10 seconds. Remove cover and, with motor on, add

1 cup ripe olives, pitted

Turn off motor as soon as olives have been drawn down into cutting blades. Pour over leeks in saucepan. Bring to a boil and simmer, covered, for 20 minutes, stirring occasionally. Serve with the baked lamb. Serves 6.

Tabbouleh

(A Parsley Salad Flavored with Mint)

Soak ½ cup cracked wheat in 1 cup water for 1 hour. Drain and press out excess liquid. (If whole wheat is used, it can easily be cracked in the blender.) Into container put

½ small onion

Fill container loosely with parsley clusters. Add water just to cover, cover, and blend on high speed for 4 seconds. Drain and empty parsley into bowl. Add the soaked wheat and mix. Into container put

1 medium tomato, coarsely cut
¾ teaspoon salt
3 tablespoons lemon juice
4 tablespoons olive oil
¼ teaspoon pepper
½ clove garlic
½ teaspoon dried mint

Cover and blend for 2 seconds. Pour dressing over salad and toss lightly. Serve 4.

Salatit Khyaar Bi Laban

Empty 1 cup yoghurt into towel. Set it in a bowl and let drain for 1 hour, squeezing towel occasionally to extract excess moisture. Into container put

1 clove garlic
1 cucumber, peeled and coarsely sliced
½ teaspoon each salt and dried mint

Cover and blend on high speed for 4 seconds. Empty into a bowl and mix with the drained yoghurt. Serves 4.

Orange Custard Pudding

Into container put

Thinly peeled rind of 1 orange
½ cup sugar
2 cups milk
3 tablespoons cornstarch

Cover and turn motor on low speed. Switch to high and blend for 20 seconds. Pour into saucepan and add 1 cup milk. Cook over low heat, stirring constantly, until thickened. Remove from heat and beat in 3 egg yolks. Turn into 6 individual dishes. In a small saucepan combine ½ cup sugar and 2 tablespoons water. Cook over low heat until syrup turns pale gold in color. Pour thin layer of the syrup over surfaces of the orange custards and chill. Serves 6.

NORWAY

Boneless Birds

Pound 1 pound very lean beef, thinly sliced, with flat side of a cleaver or heavy chopping knife until paper-thin. Into container put half of the following ingredients:

1 pound ground lean beef
1 teaspoon potato starch
½ teaspoon ginger
¼ teaspoon clove
½ cup milk

Cover and blend on high speed for 1 minute. Empty into bowl and repeat, using remaining ground beef, starch, ginger, clove, and milk. Spread beef slices with the ground mixture, roll like tiny jelly rolls, and tie with string. Put the "birds" into a frying pan with 1 inch water and add ¼ pound marrowbone, 1 stalk celery, and 1 medium onion, sliced. Bring water to a boil and cook until water has almost cooked away. Continue cooking until "birds" are browned on all sides. Remove "birds" and discard marrowbone. To juices, celery, and onion remaining in pan stir in 2 tablespoons flour. Gradu-

Norway

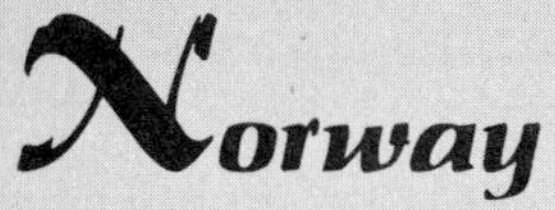

*Cherry Soup**
*Boneless Birds**
Boiled Parsley Potatoes
*Red Cabbage in Red Wine**
or
*Norwegian Fish Pudding **
with
*Sour-Cream Dill Sauce**
*Scandinavian Dark Bread**
or
*Cheese Popovers**
Beet Salad
*Wild-Rice Pancakes**

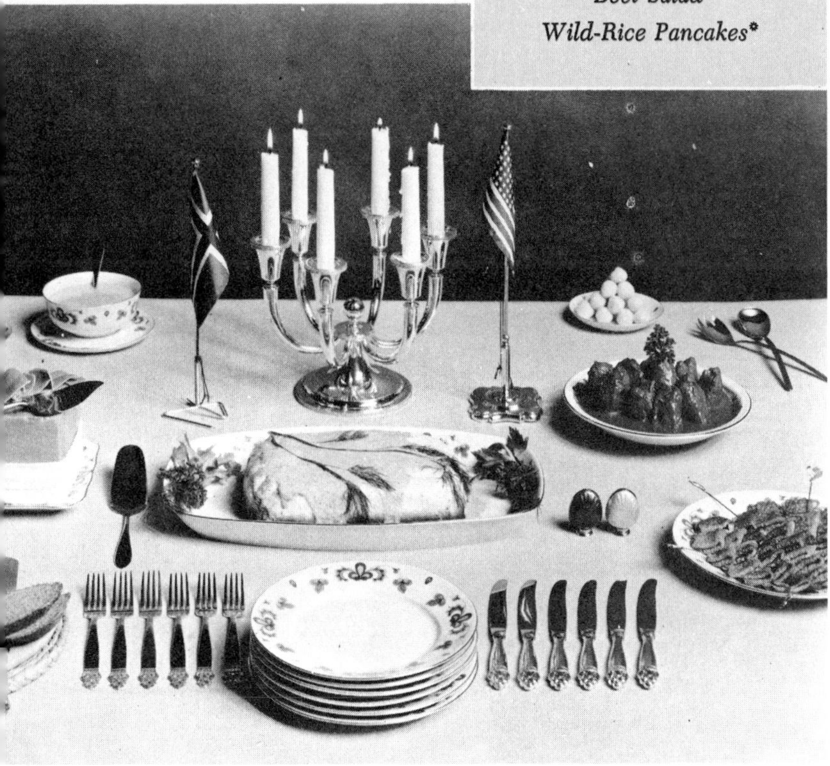

ally stir in 1 quart boiling water. Cook, stirring in all the brown bits from bottom and sides of pan. Into container put

The celery and onion from the gravy
½ cup gravy

Cover and blend on high speed for 3 seconds. Remove cover and, with motor on, gradually pour in remaining gravy. Pour gravy back into frying pan. Return the "birds" to the gravy, after removing strings, and simmer, covered, for 1 hour. Serve in a deep dish, or stack pyramid fashion as the Norwegians do. Serves 6.

Red Cabbage in Red Wine

In a saucepan melt 2 tablespoons butter or bacon drippings. Core and slice coarsely 1 medium head red cabbage. Fill container with cabbage and add water just to cover. Cover container and blend on high speed for 5 seconds, or until cabbage is shredded. Drain and empty into saucepan. Repeat until all cabbage is shredded. Sprinkle cabbage with

1 tablespoon flour
1 teaspoon salt
1 tablespoon sugar
1 teaspoon caraway seeds
1 cup red wine

Bring to a boil, cover, and simmer for 1½ hours. Serves 6.

Norwegian Fish Pudding

Into container put

1 pound raw fish fillets, cut into chunks
1 cup milk
2 tablespoons potato starch
2 eggs
¼ teaspoon nutmeg

Cover and blend on high speed for 2 minutes. Remove cover and, with motor on, pour in

About ½ cup milk, or enough to fill jar three-quarters' full

With motor still running, pour in

1 cup heavy cream

Immediately turn off motor. Pour mixture into a buttered quart mold, set mold in pan containing about 1 inch warm water, and bake in a 325° F. oven for 1 hour, or until pudding is set in center. Serve in mold, or turn out and garnish with cooked shrimp. Serve with Sour-Cream Dill Sauce. Serves 6.

Sour-Cream Dill Sauce

(For Any Poached Fish or Fish Pudding)

Into container put

1 cup commercial sour cream
1 small bunch fresh dill with stems, coarsely cut

Cover and blend on high speed for 20 seconds, Heat until lukewarm over hot water. Do not let boil. To serve cold, chill. The sauce will set in a few minutes. If desired, parsley clusters may be added along with the dill. Makes 1 cup.

Scandinavian Dark Bread

Into mixing bowl put 1 envelope dry yeast and 2½ cups lukewarm water. Let soak for 5 minutes. Stir to combine; then add 2 cups dry milk solids, 2 teaspoons salt, 1 teaspoon sugar, 2 cups stone-ground rye flour, and 2 cups stone-ground whole-wheat flour. Stir until well mixed.

Blend about 1 cup at a time for 60 seconds, or until dough turns light in color. This blending gives the bread the wonderful texture of the Scandinavian breads. When all the dough has been blended, rinse out the blender container by blending ¼ cup water and adding the liquid to the blended dough. Cover and let rise for 45 minutes. Stir down and let rise again for about 30 minutes, or until double in bulk. Stir in 2 cups stone-ground whole-wheat flour. Sprinkle pastry board with 1 cup stone-ground whole-wheat flour. Pick up dough with oiled hands and knead in the flour on the board. Put dough into an oiled bowl, oil top well, cover, and let rise for 1 hour, or until double in bulk. Knead down. Shape into 2 large or 4 small loaves. Put loaves into small, shallow, well-oiled baking dishes. Oil surface liberally and let rise again for 30 minutes. Bake in a preheated 325° F. oven for 30 minutes, or until well browned.

Cheese Popovers

Oil muffin or popover pans and heat in a 400° F. oven. Into container put

1 cup milk
2 eggs
1 cup flour

Cover and blend on low speed for 4 seconds. Switch to high and blend for 30 seconds, stopping to stir down if necessary. Fill pans half full. Drop into center of each pan ½-inch cube Norwegian cheese (*nokkelost*). Bake in the hot oven for 35 to 40 minutes, or until popovers are crisp and brown. Makes 2 dozen.

Wild-Rice Pancakes

Into container put

¼ cup wild rice

Cover and blend on high speed for 60 seconds. Add

2 eggs
1 cup milk
2 tablespoons flour
Pinch salt

Cover and blend on high speed for 30 seconds. Fry batter on a hot griddle in plenty of butter until browned on both sides, making small pancakes about 3 inches in diameter. Drain on absorbent paper; fold into quarters. Stir batter occasionally during the baking of the pancakes. Serve sprinkled with confectioners' sugar with a wedge of lemon on the side. Or serve with a favorite jam or preserved lingonberries.

NOTE: These little pancakes are excellent sprinkled with salt and served cold for an hors d'oeuvre.

THE ORIENT

Chinese Egg Rolls

Into container put

1 cup water
2 eggs
1 cup flour
½ teaspoon salt

Cover and blend on high speed for 15 seconds. Melt a small amount of butter in a 5- or 6-inch skillet. Let pan become hot. Pour in about 2 tablespoons batter and swirl pan to coat bottom with a thin layer of batter. Raise pan above heat for about 30 seconds. When pancake is set, but not brown, turn out onto a moist towel. Repeat until all but about 2 tablespoons of the batter have been used. Into container put

¼ cup water chestnuts
2 scallions, or green onions, coarsely cut
1 piece canned bamboo shoot
1 stalk celery, coarsely cut

Add water just to cover. Cover and blend on high speed for 3 to 4 seconds, or until vegetables are chopped. Drain and empty into mixing bowl. Into container put

2 eggs
1 tablespoon soy sauce
½ teaspoon salt

Cover and blend on high speed for 3 seconds. Remove cover and, with motor on, gradually add

1 pound cleaned, cooked shrimp

Continue blending until smooth, stopping to stir down if necessary. Add to vegetables and mix. Place about 1 tablespoon of the filling on ½ of each pancake. Moisten edges with remaining batter. Fold sides of pancake toward center and roll up pancake, enclosing the filling. Fry at 365° F. in hot deep fat for about 5 minutes, or until golden on all sides. Drain on absorbent paper. Serve with Plum Sauce and hot mustard. Makes 14 egg rolls.

*Chinese Egg Rolls**
*with Plum Sauce**
or
Chinese Pancakes
*with Mustard Sauce**
or
*Sweet-and-Sour Pork**
*Spinach Salad**
*Kumquat Preserve**
Almond Cakes

Plum Sauce

Into container put

1 cup plum preserve
½ cup chutney
1 tablespoon vinegar
1 tablespoon sugar

Cover and blend on high speed for 15 seconds. Turn into a small saucepan and heat to serving temperature. Makes 1½ cups.

Chinese Pancakes with Mustard Sauce

Into container put

5 eggs
1 cup diced cooked chicken
1 1-pound can chop-suey vegetables, drained

Cover and blend on high speed for 10 seconds. Fry in cakes on hot greased griddle until browned on both sides, using about ½ cup mixture for each cake. Serve with Mustard Sauce.

MUSTARD SAUCE

Into container put

1½ cups hot milk

1½ tablespoons cornstarch
2 tablespoons soft butter
1½ tablespoons dry mustard
1 teaspoon vinegar
1 teaspoon salt
1 teaspoon prepared mustard
Dash pepper

Cover and blend on high speed for 20 seconds. Cook over simmering water for 10 minutes, stirring occasionally. Makes about 1½ cups.

Sweet-and-Sour Pork

Drain and reserve syrup from 1 13½-ounce can pineapple chunks. Into container put

1 egg
3 tablespoons pineapple syrup
½ teaspoon salt
½ cup flour

Cover and blend on high speed for 10 seconds, stopping to stir down if necessary. Pour into a mixing bowl and add 1½ pounds boned leg or shoulder of pork, cut into 1-inch cubes. Toss cubes until all are coated with the batter. Fry pork cubes in hot deep fat at 365° F. for 6 to 7 minutes, or until well browned. Drain on absorbent paper. Into container put

The remaining pineapple syrup
1 medium green pepper, seeded and cut into strips
½ cup vinegar
¼ cup firmly packed brown sugar
1 tomato, quartered
1 tablespoon molasses
2 tablespoons cornstarch

Cover and blend on high speed for 15 seconds. Pour into saucepan and bring to a boil. Simmer for 5 minutes, stirring occasionally. Add pork and pineapple chunks and simmer for 15 minutes, or until pork is tender, stirring occasionally. Serve with rice. Serves 6.

Spinach Salad

Into container put

10 ounces defrosted spinach
1 tablespoon sesame seeds
1 teaspoon salt

Add water just to cover. Cover and blend on high speed for 2 seconds. Turn into saucepan and bring to a boil. Simmer for 2 minutes. Drain well. Press about 3 tablespoons each into 6 individual molds. Chill. Unmold and serve with lime or lemon slices. Serves 6.

Kumquat Preserve

Split and seed 2 pounds kumquats. Into container put

1 pound kumquats, split and seeded

Add water just to cover. Cover and blend on high speed for 4 to 5 seconds, or until fruit is finely chopped. Empty into saucepan. Repeat using remaining kumquats. Into container put

6 ounces crystallized ginger
2 limes, halved and seeded

Add water to cover. Cover and blend on high speed for 5 seconds. Add to kumquats. Bring to a boil and add 3 cups sugar. Simmer for 1 hour, or until thickened and clear, stirring occasionally. Serve as a sweet with small cakes or cookies, or pour while hot into jars and seal. Makes about 3 pints.

SPAIN

Gazpacho

Fill container to top with

1 clove garlic
4 ripe tomatoes, quartered
½ green pepper, seeded and sliced
½ small onion, peeled and sliced
1 cucumber, peeled and coarsely sliced
1 teaspoon salt

¼ teaspoon pepper
2 tablespoons olive oil
3 tablespoons wine vinegar
½ cup ice water

Cover and blend on high speed for 2 to 3 seconds only, or until vegetables are coarsely chopped. Chill or pour into serving plates and serve with an ice cube in the center of each serving. Serves 4.

Spanish Pork Chops

Coat 4 pork chops with a mixture of ¼ cup flour, ½ teaspoon salt, and ¼ teaspoon coarsely ground pepper. Brown chops slowly in a skillet in 2 tablespoons melted fat or shortening. Into container put

1 medium onion, quartered
½ cup coarsely cut celery
½ green pepper, seeded and cut into strips
½ teaspoon orégano
½ teaspoon paprika
¼ cup parsley clusters
¼ teaspoon thyme
½ bay leaf
1 No. 2 can tomatoes

Cover and blend on high speed for 10 seconds. Pour off excess fat from skillet, add tomato mixture, cover, and cook over low heat for 45 minutes. Serves 4.

Gazpacho
*Spanish Pork Chops**
Cooked Rice
*Honeyed Apples**

Honeyed Apples

Into container put

½ cup water
4 dried figs, diced
⅓ cup almonds

Cover and blend on high speed for 15 seconds, stopping to stir down if necessary. Core 6 medium apples, and peel halfway down around each apple. Fill centers of apples with the fig filling. Place apples in buttered baking dish and pour over them ½ cup honey. Bake in a preheated 350° F. oven for 30 minutes, or until apples are tender, basting occasionally with the hot honey in the pan. Arrange apples in serving dish and pour over each 1 tablespoon sherry. Serves 4.

Chapter 7 VEGETABLES

The electric blender can speed the preparation of vegetables by chopping or mincing raw vegetables, or by puréeing cooked ones. It can make wonderfully savory casseroles and creamed dishes from canned or cooked leftover vegetables to help stretch the food dollar.

Do not expect your blender to mash cooked potatoes. The correct fluffy-type mashed-potato consistency is obtained by a rotary beating action rather than by the homogenizing action of the electric blender. The blender develops the starch in the potatoes, and the result is a waxy purée rather than a fluffy mashed product. But the blender makes many other kinds of vegetable purées.

To Make a Purée

Always begin with enough liquid to cover the blades, or about ½ cup. The liquid may be water, milk, tomato juice, or consommé. Gradually add cooked vegetables, while blending on high speed, until the correct consistency of a purée is obtained. Season with salt and pepper and keep hot until ready to serve by standing the blender container in a saucepan containing a little hot water.

To Mince Small Quantities of Raw Vegetables

Blend only ½ cup coarsely cut raw vegetables such as carrots, onions, or green pepper, at a time.

To Shred Large Quantities of Raw Vegetables

Fill container loosely with coarsely cut vegetables such as cabbage, celery, carrots, green pepper, and onion, add cold water to cover vegetables, cover container, and blend for *just seconds* (about 5), or until the last piece of vegetable in the top of the container is drawn down into the blades. Drain vegetables in a sieve. For finely shredded raw vegetables, continue blending a little longer, or until vegetables are finely chopped.

Potato Pancakes

2 eggs
1 slice medium onion
1 teaspoon salt
¼ cup parsley clusters
2 cups diced raw potatoes
¼ cup flour

Break eggs into blender container. Add onion slice, salt, parsley, and half the potatoes. Cover container and turn motor on high.

Uncover container and, with motor on, add flour and remaining potatoes. Turn off motor as soon as last potato cube has been added.

Pour batter onto a hot greased griddle and cook on both sides until brown. Makes 8 pancakes.

Beans with Mushroom Sauce

Into container put

1 egg
½ cup cream or milk
1 teaspoon lemon juice
4 sprigs parsley
½ small onion
½ teaspoon salt
Dash pepper
1 can (4-ounces) sliced mushrooms, drained

Cover and blend on high speed for 10 seconds. Pour over 2 cups cooked green beans. Cook over simmering water, stirring occasionally, for 10 minutes. Serves 4.

Orange Beets

Into container put

Pulp of 2 oranges
1 tablespoon butter
4 tablespoons brown sugar
1 tablespoon cornstarch
¼ teaspoon salt
Dash pepper

Cover and blend on high speed for 20 seconds. Pour into saucepan and cook over simmering water for 10 minutes, stirring occasionally. Add 2½ cups cooked sliced beets. Continue cooking until beets are hot. Serves 6.

Savory Beets

Into container put

½ cup cooked sliced beets
3 tablespoons vinegar
⅛ teaspoon ground cloves
½ teaspoon salt
¼ cup sugar
1 thin slice medium onion
2 tablespoons soft butter

Cover and blend on high speed for 10 seconds. Pour over 2 cups cooked sliced beets. Simmer, stirring frequently, for 15 to 20 minutes. Serves 4.

Broccoli Loaf

(Or Spinach or Cauliflower)

Into container put

3 cups cooked chopped vegetables
1 cup vegetable water

Cover and blend on high speed for 5 seconds, or until last piece of vegetable is drawn down into blades. Empty into bowl. Into container put

2 eggs
1 medium onion, sliced
2 stalks celery, coarsely cut
½ cup tomato juice or consommé
¼ cup melted butter
1 teaspoon salt
Dash pepper
2 slices dry bread, broken

Cover and blend on high speed for 20 seconds. Add to chopped vegetables, mix well, and turn into a 1½-quart buttered casserole. Bake in a preheated 325° F. oven for 40 minutes. Serve hot with Cheese Sauce or Hollandaise Sauce. Serves 6.

Creamed Cabbage

Into container put

4 cups coarsely sliced cabbage

Fill container with cold water to 2 inches from top. Cover and blend on high speed for 2 seconds. Drain well and turn shredded cabbage into saucepan. Into container put

¾ cup hot milk
2 tablespoons soft butter
2 tablespoons flour
1 teaspoon dehydrated minced onion
¼ teaspoon celery seed
1 teaspoon salt

Cover and blend on high speed for 10 seconds. Add to cabbage and cook over low heat 15 minutes, or until cabbage is tender, stirring occasionally. Serves 4.

Sweet-and-Sour Red Cabbage

Follow recipe for shredding Coleslaw, using:

½ medium cabbage
1 apple, coarsely cut and cored
1 medium onion

Empty drained mixture into saucepan and add 1½ teaspoons caraway seeds, 1 tablespoon sugar, 1 cup water, and 1 cup wine vinegar. Cover and simmer for 1 hour. Serves 4.

Glazed Carrots

Into container put

2 cups raw sliced carrots
½ cup water
2 tablespoons melted butter
½ teaspoon salt
⅛ teaspoon pepper
1 tablespoon sugar
1 tablespoon cornstarch
1 tablespoon lemon juice

Cover and blend on high speed for 10 seconds, or until carrots are finely ground. Pour into saucepan and cook over low heat for 25 minutes, stirring occasionally. Serves 6.

Carrot Custard

Into container put

2 cups cooked sliced carrots*

* 2 cups any cooked vegetables may be used, or 1 1-pound can vegetables, drained.

3 eggs
¼ cup milk
1 small onion, halved
¼ cup parsley sprigs
3 tablespoons melted butter
2 tablespoons flour
1½ teaspoons salt
¼ teaspoon pepper

Cover and blend on high speed for 10 seconds. Turn into 6 buttered 5-ounce custard cups. Place in pan with 1 inch hot water. Bake in preheated 350° F. oven for 45 minutes. Unmold and garnish with asparagus. Serves 6. May be baked in a 4-cup mold if desired.

Cauliflower Soufflé

Cook 1 medium head cauliflower (about 1½ pounds), covered, in 1 inch boiling water for 15 to 20 minutes, or until tender.

Into container break

2 soda crackers

Cover and blend on high speed for 5 seconds. Sprinkle crumbs onto bottom and sides of a greased 2-quart soufflé dish. Into container put

⅓ cup diced Parmesan cheese

Cover and blend on high speed for 6 seconds. Empty crumbs out onto waxed paper and set aside. Break cooked cauliflower into pieces and put into container. Add

½ cup milk

Cover and blend on high speed for 20 seconds, or until smooth, stopping to stir down if necessary. Add

1 teaspoon salt
4 egg yolks
⅛ teaspoon pepper
¼ cup flour
¼ cup soft butter

Cover and blend on high speed for 10 seconds, or until smooth. Fold in 4 egg whites, stiffly beaten, and the grated cheese. Turn into prepared soufflé dish and bake in a preheated 350° F. oven for 40 to 45 minutes. Serve immediately. Serves 6.

Corn Pie

Line a 9-inch pie pan with pastry. Make a standing fluted edge. Into container put

3 eggs
1 slice bread, torn
3 tablespoons soft butter
1 teaspoon sugar
½ teaspoon salt
¼-inch slice small onion
5 sprigs parsley
1½ cups whole-kernel corn

Cover and blend on high speed for 20 seconds. Pour into pastry-lined pan. Top with

½ cup (1 slice bread) blender-made bread crumbs
½ cup blender-grated cheese

Bake in a 450° F. oven for 10 minutes. Lower heat to 350° F. and bake for 30 minutes longer. Serves 6.

Corn Fritters

Into container put

1 cup corn, cut from cob, or 1 cup frozen or canned corn
1 egg
½ teaspoon salt
½ teaspoon baking powder
¼ cup milk
¼ cup flour

Cover and blend on high speed for 15 seconds. Fry in a skillet in 1 inch hot shortening until well browned. Drop batter in by the tablespoonful. Makes 1 dozen small fritters.

Baked Corn

Into container break

8 soda crackers

Cover and blend on high speed for 6 seconds, or until crackers are crumbed. Empty crackers into waxed paper. Into container put

1 can (16 ounces) cream-style corn
2 eggs
½ teaspoon salt
¼ teaspoon pepper
¼ green pepper, cut into strips
½ small onion

Cover and blend on high speed for 20 seconds. Pour into a buttered 1-quart casserole or baking dish, top with crumbs, and dot with butter. Bake in a preheated 325° F. oven for 45 minutes. Serves 6.

Scalloped Corn

Into container tear

1 slice bread

Cover and blend on high speed for 5 seconds. Empty crumbs onto waxed paper. Into container put

1 medium onion, sliced
1 green pepper, seeded and coarsely sliced
1 cup water

Cover and blend on high speed for 3 seconds. Empty vegetables into sieve to drain. Sauté the chopped vegetables until soft but not browned in 2 tablespoons butter. Into container put

1 teaspoon salt
⅛ teaspoon pepper
2 tablespoons flour
1 cup hot milk
1 tablespoon soft butter
¼ teaspoon cayenne
¼ teaspoon dry mustard
1 package (10 ounces) defrosted corn, or 2 cups fresh-corn kernels
1 egg
1 slice bread, torn

Cover and blend on high speed for 5 seconds. Empty into buttered casserole. Stir in onion-and-green-pepper mixture. Sprinkle with reserved bread crumbs and dot with butter. Bake in a preheated 375° F. oven for 20 minutes or until bubbly and brown. Serves 4.

Baked Eggplant

Peel 1 medium eggplant. Slice, and cook in boiling salted water for 10 minutes, or until tender. Drain. Into container tear

1 slice bread

Cover and blend on high speed for 6 seconds, or until bread is crumbed. Empty onto waxed paper. Into container put

The drained eggplant
¼ cup cream
2 tablespoons soft butter or cooking oil
½ small onion
1 thin slice garlic clove
2 eggs
½ teaspoon salt
Dash pepper
1 teaspoon lemon juice
1 slice bread

Cover and blend on high speed for 20 seconds. Pour into a greased 1-quart casserole and top with the bread crumbs. Bake in a preheated 325° F. oven for 30 minutes. Serves 6.

Rice-Stuffed Peppers

Cut a thin slice from stem end of 4 green peppers. Discard seeds and white pulp. Parboil in covered pan with 1 cup water and 1 teaspoon salt for 5 minutes. Drain well. Into container put

1 slice bread, torn
1 medium onion, quartered
2 fresh tomatoes, quartered, or 2 whole canned tomatoes
1 teaspoon paprika
1 teaspoon chili powder
1 teaspoon salt
1 thin slice garlic

Cover and blend on high speed for 10 seconds. Pour sauce over 2 cups cooked rice. Mix, and stuff peppers. Dot each with 1 teaspoon butter. Arrange in baking pan, cover, and bake in a preheated 350° F. oven for 40 minutes. Serves 4.

Lima-Bean-and-Rice Casserole

In a 1½-quart buttered casserole combine 2 cups cooked Lima beans and two cups cooked rice. Into container put

½-inch slice green pepper
2 stalks celery, coarsely cut
1¼ cups tomato juice
2 tablespoons melted butter
1 teaspoon salt
⅛ teaspoon pepper
¼-inch slice medium onion

Cover and blend on high speed for 10 seconds. Pour over rice and beans and bake in a preheated 350° F. oven for 30 minutes. (If desired, cover casserole before baking with bread crumbs and dot with butter.) Serves 4.

Baked Potatoes with Cheese-Chive Sauce

Split and open 4 baked potatoes. Flake pulp lightly with a fork and keep hot. Into container put

8 ounces large-curd cottage cheese
¼ cup milk
½ teaspoon salt
Dash pepper
1 tablespoon cut green-onion tops or chives

Cover and blend on high speed for 6 seconds. Spoon sauce over hot potatoes and, if desired, sprinkle with more chopped-onion tops or chives. Serves 4.

Potato Pudding

Peel and slice 4 medium potatoes and 1 onion. Fill container with the prepared vegetables. Add water to cover, cover, and blend on high speed for 5 seconds, or until vegetables are finely chopped. Empty into sieve to drain and repeat until all vegetables are chopped. Into container put

3 eggs

(*see over*)

¼ cup parsley
1½ teaspoons salt
¼ teaspoon pepper
½ cup flour
¼ cup melted shortening
½ cup milk

Cover and blend on high speed for 10 seconds. Pour batter over potatoes, mix well, and turn into greased 1½-quart casserole. Bake in a preheated 350° F. oven for 1 hour. Serves 6.

Potato Puff

Into container put

½ cup milk
3 eggs
¼ cup parsley clusters
1 small onion, halved
½ green pepper, cut in strips
1½ teaspoons salt
¼ teaspoon pepper
¼ cup melted butter
1 cup diced Cheddar cheese

Cover and blend on high speed for 5 seconds. Add, 1 cup at a time,

3 medium potatoes, peeled and diced

Cover and blend on high speed until potatoes are finely grated. Pour into a buttered 1½-quart casserole and bake in a preheated 350° F. oven for 1 hour. Serves 6.

Sweet Potatoes Dixie

Into container put

Pulp from 2 oranges
¼ cup melted butter
2 tablespoons rum or sherry
½ teaspoon salt
¼ cup milk
¼ cup brown sugar
¼ teaspoon nutmeg

Cover and blend on high speed for 10 seconds. Remove cover and, with motor on, drop in, 1 at a time,

About 4 cooked sweet potatoes

Stop to stir down if necessary and stop adding potatoes when mixture becomes too thick to blend. Do not overwork motor. Turn mixture into a buttered 1-quart casserole and bake in a preheated 350° F. oven for 30 minutes. Serves 4.

Spiced Sweet-Potato Casserole

Into container put

½ cup cream or milk
2 eggs
¼ cup melted butter
½ teaspoon salt
½ teaspoon cinnamon
½ teaspoon ginger
½ cup brown sugar
1 cup diced raw sweet potatoes

Cover and turn motor on high. Remove cover and gradually add

2 cups diced raw sweet potatoes

Pour into a buttered 1-quart casserole and bake in a preheated 325° F. oven for 45 minutes. Serve hot. Serves 6.

Sweet-Potato-and-Date Casserole

Into container put

½ cup cream or milk
3 eggs
2 tablespoons rum or sherry
½ teaspoon cinnamon
¾ teaspoon salt
¼ cup melted butter

Cover and turn motor on high speed. Remove cover and add

¾ cup pitted dates

Push down into blades, 1 at a time, until mixture in container reaches top,

About 5 small cooked sweet potatoes

Pour mixture into a 4-cup buttered baking dish and cover top with halved pecans. Bake in a preheated 350° F. oven for 30 minutes. Serves 6.

Spanish-Rice Ring

Into container put

1 1-pound can whole tomatoes
1 small onion, halved
½ clove garlic
1 4-ounce can pimientos, drained
1 green pepper, seeded and cut into strips
½ cup diced Cheddar cheese
3 dashes Tabasco
1½ teaspoons salt
¼ cup melted butter

Cover and blend on high speed for 20 seconds. Add to 4½ cups cooked rice. Mix well and turn into a well-greased 1½-quart ring mold. Place in pan with 1 inch warm water. Bake in a preheated 350° F. oven for 1¼ hours. Cool for 5 minutes and turn out from mold. Fill with creamed vegetables. Serves 6.

Spinach Soufflé

Cook 1 10-ounce package frozen spinach* according to package directions. Drain well. Into container put

The spinach
5 egg yolks
4 tablespoons flour
4 tablespoons softened butter
1 teaspoon salt
⅛ teaspoon pepper
¾ cup hot milk

Cover and blend on high speed for 15 seconds. Pour into saucepan and cook over low heat, stirring until thick. Remove from heat, cool, and fold in 5 beaten egg whites. Pour into a 1½-quart casserole.

* Other vegetables in same weight package may be substituted to make other soufflés.

Bake in a preheated 375° F. oven for 30 minutes. Serve immediately. Serves 4.

Mexican Succotash

Into a buttered 1-quart baking dish put 1½ cups cooked baby Lima beans and 1 cup cooked whole-kernel corn, drained. Into container put

- 2 eggs
- 2 tablespoons tomato catchup
- ¼ cup milk
- 1 thick slice medium onion
- 4 1-inch strips green pepper
- 1 teaspoon salt
- ⅛ teaspoon pepper
- ½ teaspoon chili powder
- 3 tablespoons soft butter

Cover and blend on high speed for 10 seconds. Pour mixture over beans and corn, stir to mix, and bake in a preheated 325° F. oven for 45 minutes. Serve hot. Serves 4.

Stuffed Tomatoes

Wash 6 medium tomatoes and scoop out centers. Turn tomatoes upside down to drain. Into container put

- 2 cups cooked spinach, well drained
- ½ cup milk
- 3 tablespoons flour
- 3 tablespoons soft butter
- ½ cup diced Cheddar cheese
- ¾ teaspoon salt

Cover and blend on high speed for 10 seconds, or until spinach is coarsely chopped. Turn into saucepan and cook, stirring, until thick. Sprinkle the tomatoes inside with salt and pepper and fill with spinach mixture. Top with

- ¼ cup (½ slice bread) blender-made bread crumbs
- ¼ cup blender-grated cheese

Bake in a shallow pan in a preheated 350° F. oven for 15 to 20 minutes, or until thoroughly hot. Serves 6.

Vegetable Casserole

Butter a shallow casserole and line the bottom with 1 package frozen vegetable, cooked, such as baby Lima beans, broccoli, asparagus, string beans, or cauliflower. Into container put

¼ cup peanuts or cashew nuts.

Cover and blend on high speed for 6 seconds. Empty nuts onto piece of waxed paper. Make Mushroom Sauce and pour over vegetables in casserole. Sprinkle with chopped nuts and bake in a preheated 350° F. oven for 30 minutes. Serves 3.

Orange Yams

In a baking dish arrange 1 can (1 pound, 10 ounces) sweet potatoes, drained, reserving ½ cup syrup. Dot with 2 tablespoons butter. Into container put

½ cup syrup from the potatoes
Pinch ginger
Pinch mace
¼ orange, seeded, including peel
¼ teaspoon salt
1 tablespoon brown sugar

Cover and blend on high speed until orange is finely cut. Pour over potatoes and bake in a preheated 350° F. oven for 1 hour. Serves 4.

Chapter 8 SAVORY SAUCES

SAUCES

There need never be another lumpy cream sauce or gravy! In addition to smoothing and blending these basic sauces, the electric blender makes the more glamorous sauces, generally considered too difficult for the average homemaker to attempt, a cinch.

From a simple white sauce and its many variations, to hearty barbecue and spaghetti sauces, to delicate wine and egg sauces—the electric blender makes short work of them all. Such kitchen chores as the tedious chopping of vegetables or the pressing of cooked mixtures through a fine sieve are literally accomplished in seconds.

MAYONNAISE

Mayonnaise and a variety of mayonnaise sauces for seafood or salad greens can be made in an electric blender in seconds. Making your own mayonnaise has many advantages, for you can change the flavor to suit the occasion or your taste. You can add a clove of garlic along with the egg and mustard to make the famous sauce of Brittany—Sauce Aioli. You can add curry powder or herbs, tomato paste or other savory ingredients, to change both flavor and color of the mayonnaise. Here are some very excellent classic sauces made by blending various ingredients with the basic Mayonnaise in the container.

Mayonnaise

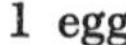

1 egg
½ teaspoon dry mustard
½ teaspoon salt
2 tablespoons vinegar
1 cup salad oil

Break egg into blender container. Add mustard, salt, and vinegar.

Add ¼ cup of the oil. Cover and turn motor on low speed.

Immediately uncover and pour in remaining oil in a steady stream. Makes 1¼ cups.

Homemade mayonnaise may be flavored to taste with garlic or herbs. Lemon juice may be used instead of vinegar. Half olive oil and half corn or peanut oil makes a delicious dressing.

Celery-Seed Mayonnaise

(For Fruit Salads)

Into container put

- ⅓ cup honey
- 1 teaspoon celery seed
- 1 egg
- ½ teaspoon salt
- 2 tablespoons lemon juice
- ¼ cup salad oil

Cover container and turn motor on low speed. Immediately remove cover and add in a steady stream

- ¾ cup salad oil

Turn off motor when last drop of oil has been added. Makes 1½ cups.

Curry Mayonnaise

(For Fruit or Fish)

Into container put

- 1 teaspoon curry powder
- ¼ teaspoon ginger
- 2 tablespoons lime juice
- 1 egg
- ½ small clove garlic
- ¼ very small onion
- 2 tablespoons honey
- ¼ cup salad oil

Cover container and turn motor on low speed. Immediately remove cover and add in a steady stream

- ¾ cup salad oil

Turn off motor when last drop of oil has been added. Makes 1⅓ cups.

Green Mayonnaise

(For Sliced Tomatoes or Cucumbers)

Into container put

- ½ small clove garlic
- 1 tablespoon fresh dill
- 1 tablespoon chopped chives or scallions
- 1 egg
- ½ teaspoon salt
- 1 teaspoon dry mustard
- 2 tablespoons wine vinegar
- ¼ cup salad oil

Cover and turn motor on low speed. Immediately remove cover and add in a steady stream

- ¾ cup salad oil

Turn off motor when the last drop of oil has been added. Makes 1¼ cups.

Honey Mayonnaise

(For Fruit Salads)

Into container put

1 egg
1 tablespoon honey
¼ teaspoon ginger
1 teaspoon dry mustard
2 tablespoons lemon juice
⅛ teaspoon garlic powder
½ teaspoon salt
1 drop red food coloring
¼ cup salad oil

Cover and turn motor on low speed. Immediately remove cover and add in a steady stream

¾ cup salad oil

Turn motor off when last drop of oil has been added. Fold in some chopped chives if desired. Makes 1¼ cups.

Sauce Aioli

(For Grilled Lamb and Other Meats, If You Like Garlic!)

Add 4 cloves garlic to 1¼ cups blender Mayonnaise. Stir to combine, cover container, and blend on high speed for 10 seconds.

Sauce Cappon Magro

(For Fish Salads)

To 1¼ cups blender Mayonnaise add

1 cup parsley clusters
1 clove garlic
1 tablespoon capers
6 green olives, pitted
Pinch fennel

Stir to combine, cover container, and blend on high speed for 6 seconds. Makes 1½ cups.

Green Goddess Sauce

(For Seafood or Salad Greens)

Make Mayonnaise and leave in container. Add
1 clove garlic
2 anchovy fillets
4 green onions with tops, coarsely cut
¼ cup parsley clusters
1 tablespoon lemon juice
1 tablespoon tarragon vinegar
¼ teaspoon coarsely ground pepper
Cover and blend on high speed for 10 seconds, or until vegetables are finely ground. Makes 1½ cups.

SOUR-CREAM GREEN GODDESS

Fold ½ cup sour cream into Green Goddess Sauce.

Sauce Gribiche

(For Head Lettuce, or a Dip for Smoked Fish)

To 1¼ cups blender Mayonnaise add
2 tablespoons parsley clusters
1 teaspoon dill weed
1 small sour pickle, coarsely cut
1 tablespoon coarsely cut onion
1 tablespoon lemon juice
3 drops Tabasco
Stir to combine, cover container, and blend on high speed for 6 seconds. Add, 1 at a time,
3 hard-cooked eggs
Push each egg down into the blades with a rubber spatula. Blend each egg for 1 second only. Makes about 3 cups.

Lamaise Sauce

(For Seafood or Salad Greens)

Make blender Mayonnaise and leave in container. Add
1 cup chili sauce

¼ cup pickle relish
1 canned pimiento
1 stalk celery, coarsely cut
2 green onions with tops, coarsely cut
1 ½-inch slice green pepper
1 teaspoon dry mustard

Cover and blend on high speed for 10 seconds, or until vegetables are finely ground. If desired, mix with ½ cup sour cream. Makes about 3¼ cups.

Sauce Michele

(For Sliced Cold Chicken or Chicken Salad)

To 1¼ cups blender Mayonnaise add

1 tablespoon capers
½ stalk celery, coarsely cut
1 slice medium onion, about ¼ inch thick
2 tablespoons parsley clusters
¼ teaspoon marjoram
½ small clove garlic

Stir to combine, cover container, and blend on high speed for 6 seconds. Makes 1½ cups.

Sauce Ravigote

(For Poached or Sautéed Fish Fillets or Trout)

In a saucepan combine

2 tablespoons capers
2 tablespoons parsley
1 clove garlic
2 tablespoons coarsely cut onion
⅓ cup white wine
1 tablespoon lemon juice

Bring ingredients to a boil and simmer for 15 minutes. Add the cooked mixture to 1¼ cups blender Mayonnaise. Stir to combine and blend on high speed for 3 seconds. Turn off motor, stir, and blend again for 5 seconds. Push down into blades

1 hard-cooked egg

and blend for just 1 second. Makes 1½ cups.

Sauce Niçoise

(For Cooked Seafood or Salad Greens)

To 1¼ cups blender Mayonnaise add

½ cup green pepper, seeded and coarsely cut
¼ cup tomato paste
1 teaspoon tarragon
1 tablespoon chopped chives

Stir to combine, cover container, and blend on high speed for 6 seconds. Makes 1½ cups.

Sauce Rémoulade

(For Fried Fish or Seafood)

To 1¼ cups blender Mayonnaise add

1 tablespoon capers
¼ cup coarsely cut sour pickles
½ teaspoon dry mustard
1 tablespoon parsley clusters
1 teaspoon tarragon

Stir to combine, cover container, and blend on high speed for 6 seconds. Makes 1½ cups.

Sauce à la Ritz

(For Salad Greens, or a Dip for Raw Vegetables)

To 1¼ cups blender Mayonnaise add

¼ teaspoon Worcestershire sauce
1 fresh tomato, peeled and quartered
1 tablespoon chili sauce
1 clove garlic
2 tablespoons parsley clusters

Stir to combine, cover container, and blend on high speed for 6 seconds. Makes about 1¾ cups.

Sauce Tartare

(For Fried Fish or Seafood)

To 1¼ cups blender Mayonnaise add

1 tablespoon parsley clusters
2 cloves garlic
5 sweet gherkins
3 pitted olives
1 teaspoon tarragon
¼ teaspoon coarsely ground pepper

Stir to combine, cover container, and blend on high speed for 6 seconds. Makes 1½ cups.

Skordalia

(A Greek Version of Aioli to Serve with Boiled Beef, Boiled Potatoes, Carrots, Artichokes, Hard-Cooked Eggs, and Poached Snails)

To 1¼ cups blender Mayonnaise add
- ½ cup blanched almonds
- 2 cloves garlic
- 2 tablespoons parsley clusters

Stir to combine, cover container, and blend on high speed for 15 seconds. Makes 1½ cups.

Sour-Cream Mayonnaise

(For Coleslaw and Tossed Greens)

To 1¼ cups blender Mayonnaise add
- 1 cup sour cream
- 2 tablespoons lemon juice

Cover container and blend on high speed for 5 seconds. Makes about 2 cups.

Thousand Island Sauce

(For Head Lettuce)

Make blender Mayonnaise and leave in container. Add
- ¼ cup chili sauce
- 1 slice medium onion
- 1 stalk celery with leaves, coarsely cut
- ¼ cup stuffed olives
- 4 gherkins
- 2 tablespoons parsley clusters
- 1 ½-inch slice green pepper
- 1 teaspoon paprika

Cover and blend on high speed for 10 seconds, or until vegetables are coarsely chopped. Remove cover and, with motor on, drop in
- 1 hard-cooked egg yolk

Turn off motor immediately. Makes about 2 cups.

Quick Sauce Verte

(For Cold Salmon and Smoked Fish)

To 1¼ cups blender Mayonnaise add

1½ tablespoons chopped chives
1 teaspoon tarragon
¼ cup parsley clusters
1 teaspoon dill weed

Stir to combine, cover container, and blend on high speed for 6 seconds. Makes 1½ cups.

HOLLANDAISE SAUCE

One of the newest cooking techniques developed for the electric blender is the making of a quick Hollandaise Sauce that cannot curdle. All you do is blend hot melted butter into egg yolks, and the sauce is ready to serve—on cooked broccoli, asparagus, cauliflower; on poached eggs; or with poached salmon and other delicate fish. Both recipes are based on the classic proportions for this sauce, but one makes a larger quantity. Select the one that fits the number of servings desired.

Hollandaise Sauce for Four Servings

In a small saucepan heat to bubbling—but do not let brown—½ cup (1 stick) butter. Into container put

3 egg yolks
2 tablespoons lemon juice
¼ teaspoon salt
Pinch cayenne

Cover container and turn motor on low speed. *Immediately* remove cover and pour in the hot butter in a steady stream. When all butter is added, turn off motor. Makes ¾ cup.

Hollandaise Sauce for Six Servings

In a small container heat to bubbling—but do not let brown—½ pound butter (2 sticks). Into container put

4 egg yolks
2 tablespoons lemon juice
¼ teaspoon salt
Pinch cayenne

Cover container and turn motor on low speed. *Immediately* remove cover and pour in the hot butter in a steady stream. When all butter is added, turn off motor. Makes 1¼ cups.

NOTE: Serve Hollandaise Sauce immediately or keep warm by setting the container into a saucepan containing 2 inches of hot water. Should the sauce become too thick to pour, return the container to the blender, add 1 tablespoon or more of hot water, and blend briefly. For a thinner sauce, heat 2 tablespoons water with the butter.

Whole-Egg Hollandaise

Use 2 whole eggs in place of the 3 egg yolks.

Sauce Aurorian

(For Cold Fish, Chicken, or Vegetable Mousses)

Into ¾ cup blender Hollandaise Sauce fold 3 tablespoons mayonnaise and ½ cup whipped cream. Store in refrigerator and serve cold. Makes 1½ cups.

Sauce Maltaise

(For Cooked Vegetables—Especially Carrots and Beets)

Into ¾ cup blender Hollandaise Sauce stir 1 tablespoon orange juice and 1 to 2 teaspoons grated orange rind.

Sauce Mousseline

(For Fish, Eggs, or Vegetables)

Into ¾ cup blender Hollandaise Sauce fold ½ cup heavy cream, whipped. Makes 1¼ cups.

Sauce Béarnaise

(For Broiled Meats)

In a small saucepan combine

- 2 tablespoons white wine
- 1 tablespoon tarragon vinegar
- 2 teaspoons chopped fresh tarragon or 1 teaspoon dried tarragon
- 2 teaspoons chopped shallots or onion
- ¼ teaspoon freshly ground black pepper

Bring liquid to a boil and cook rapidly until almost all liquid disappears. Pour remaining mixture into ¾ cup blender Hollandaise Sauce, cover, and blend on high speed for 6 seconds. Makes about 1 cup.

Sauce Choron

(For Grilled or Sautéed Meats)

Make blender Sauce Béarnaise, adding, along with the cooked ingredients, 1 tablespoon tomato paste. Makes about 1 cup.

BASIC

Medium White Sauce

Into container put

- 1 cup hot milk
- 2 tablespoons flour
- 2 tablespoons soft butter

Cover and blend on high speed for 10 seconds. Pour into saucepan and cook over low heat for 3 minutes, stirring occasionally. Or cook over simmering water for 7 minutes, stirring occasionally.

Season to taste with salt and pepper. Or pour immediately over other ingredients in a casserole for a dish to be baked. Makes 1 cup.

THIN WHITE SAUCE—A base for cream soups.

Use only 1 tablespoon flour and 1 tablespoon soft butter. Makes 1 cup.

THICK WHITE SAUCE—A base for croquettes and fish, meat or vegetable rings.

Use 3 tablespoons flour and 3 tablespoons soft butter. Makes 1 cup.

CHEESE SAUCE

Add, along with other ingredients, 1/4 pound sharp Cheddar cheese, diced, 1/4 teaspoon dry mustard, 1/4 teaspoon paprika, and a dash of Tabasco. Makes 1 1/4 cups.

CHICKEN À LA KING SAUCE

To 1 cup hot Thick White Sauce stir in 1/2 cup cream, 1 canned pimiento, sliced, and 1 tablespoon dry sherry. Makes 1 1/3 cups.

HORSE-RADISH SAUCE

To 1 cup hot Thick White Sauce, stir in 1/2 cup cream, 1/4 teaspoon sugar, 1/4 cup prepared horse-radish, drained, and salt and pepper to taste. Makes 1 3/4 cups.

MOCK HOLLANDAISE

To 1 cup hot Medium White Sauce stir in 2 cups mayonnaise, 1 tablespoon lemon juice, and salt and Tabasco to taste. Makes 3 cups.

TOMATO SAUCE

To 1 cup hot Medium White Sauce blend in 6 tablespoons tomato paste and salt and pepper to taste. Makes 1 1/3 cups.

CREOLE SAUCE

To Tomato Sauce, stir in 1/4 cup each chopped celery and green pepper and 2 tablespoons minced onion. Add salt and pepper to taste and simmer over low heat for 30 minutes, or until vegetables are tender. Makes 2 cups.

CHICKEN VELOUTÉ SAUCE

Make a Medium White Sauce or Thick White Sauce, substituting chicken broth for the milk. Add a pinch each of nutmeg, salt, and pepper to taste. Makes 1 cup.

SAUCE BÉCHAMEL

Make a Medium White Sauce. Add pinch of nutmeg, salt, and pepper to taste. Add 1 small onion, minced, and pinch of thyme. Cook over low heat for 30 minutes, stirring occasionally. Makes 1 cup.

MUSHROOM SAUCE

Make a Thick White Sauce, adding to the container, along with the hot milk, 1 4-ounce can cooked mushrooms, with the juice. Makes 1½ cups.

CREAM SAUCE

To 1 cup hot Thick White Sauce or Sauce Béchamel, stir in ½ cup heavy cream. Makes 1½ cups.

MORNAY SAUCE

Make a Medium White Sauce or Sauce Béchamel, adding to container along with milk, 2 tablespoons each diced Gruyère and Parmesan cheese. Correct seasoning with salt and pepper, and cook as directed. Before using, stir in bit by bit, 2 tablespoons butter. Makes 1⅓ cups.

POULETTE SAUCE

Make a thick Velouté Sauce, adding to container along with the hot chicken broth 2 tablespoons parsley clusters. When sauce is cooked, correct seasoning with salt and pepper and stir in few drops lemon juice and 2 tablespoons butter. Makes about 1¼ cups.

NEWBURG SAUCE

To 1 cup thick Sauce Béchamel, stir in 1 egg yolk beaten with ¼ cup heavy cream and 2 tablespoons dry sherry. Makes 1½ cups.

SAUCE SUPREME

To 1 cup hot thick Chicken Velouté Sauce, stir in ¼ cup heavy cream. Makes 1¼ cups.

FROM A CAN

Cheese Sauce

(For Seafood au Gratin)

Into container put

1 10½ ounce can condensed cream of celery soup
¼ cup milk
½ cup diced Cheddar cheese
1 small onion, halved
Dash Tabasco
1 tablespoon softened butter

Cover and blend on high speed for 15 seconds. Pour into saucepan and heat over low heat to serving temperature. Makes about 1½ cups.

Country-Style Cream Sauce

(For Chicken)

Into container put

1 can condensed cream of chicken soup
¼ cup light cream or milk
¼ cup parsley clusters
1 thin slice garlic

Cover container and blend on high speed for 10 seconds. Empty into saucepan, bring to a boil, and cook over low heat for 10 minutes. Makes 1¼ cups.

Quick Mushroom Sauce

Into container put

1 3-ounce can cooked mushrooms
½ cup sour cream
½ cup hot beef consommé
2 tablespoons soft butter
2 tablespoons flour

Cover and blend on high speed for 15 seconds. Turn into saucepan and cook over simmering water for 15 minutes, stirring occasionally. Makes 1½ cups.

Sauce Piquant

(For Fish)

Into container put

1 can condensed cream of celery soup
¼ cup water
½ teaspoon dry mustard
1 tablespoon cider vinegar

Cover container and blend on high speed for 10 seconds. Remove cover and, with rubber spatula, push down into blades

1 hard-cooked egg

Immediately turn off motor. Set container into a pan of simmering water and heat without boiling. If desired, fold in 2 tablespoons sweet-pickle relish just before serving. Makes 1½ cups.

Zesty Vegetable Sauce

(For Cooked Asparagus, Green Beans and Mixed Peas and Onions, or Meat and Fish Loaves)

Into container put

1 small onion, halved
1 tablespoon soft butter
1 can (10½ ounces) condensed cream of mushroom soup
⅓ cup milk

Cover container and blend on high speed for 10 seconds. Remove cover and drop in

¼ cup pitted ripe olives, or 4 large olives

Turn off motor immediately. Pour into saucepan and heat, stirring often. Just before serving stir in ¼ cup room-temperature sour cream. ⅛ teaspoon tarragon may also be added. Makes 1¾ cups.

BREAD

Bread Sauce

(For Roast Poultry)

In a saucepan heat 1 cup milk, 2 tablespoons butter, and 1 small onion, sliced. Into container put

3 slices thin-sliced or 2 slices regular bread, torn
1/8 teaspoon clove
1/2 teaspoon salt
1/4 teaspoon paprika
Pinch cayenne

Cover container and blend on high speed for 6 seconds. Remove cover and gradually pour in the hot-milk mixture. Set container into pan of simmering water to keep hot until ready to serve. Makes 1 1/2 cups.

Cream Bread Sauce

Into container tear

1 slice bread, trimmed

Add

1 cup hot cream
2 tablespoons soft butter
1/4 teaspoon salt
Dash pepper

Cover and blend on high speed for 10 seconds. Pour into a saucepan and heat to boiling, stirring constantly. Makes 1 1/4 cups.

Cheese-Bread Sauce

In a small saucepan heat 1 cup milk, 2 tablespoons butter, 1/4 teaspoon salt, and 1/8 teaspoon cayenne. Into container tear

2 slices bread, trimmed

Add

1 cup Cheddar cheese, diced
The hot-milk mixture

Cover and blend on high speed for 20 seconds. Makes about 2 cups.

Mushroom-Bread Sauce

In a small saucepan heat

- 1 cup milk
- 2 tablespoons butter
- 1 slice medium onion
- ¼ teaspoon nutmeg
- ½ teaspoon salt
- ½ teaspoon paprika

Into container tear

- 3 slices regular bread or 4 slices thin-sliced, trimmed

Add

- The hot-milk mixture

Cover and blend on high speed for 15 seconds. Remove cover and, with motor on add

- 4 ounces canned mushrooms, drained, or 4 ounces sautéed fresh mushrooms

Continue to blend for 4 seconds longer. Makes about 2 cups.

Butter Sauce

(For Vegetables)

Into container put

- ½ cup (1 stick) soft butter
- 1 tablespoon lemon juice
- 1½ teaspoons grated lemon rind

Cover container and blend on high speed for 20 seconds. Set container into saucepan containing simmering water until butter is melted. Makes ½ cup. If desired, add one or a combination of the following:

- 2 teaspoons chopped chives or dill
- 1 tablespoon parsley clusters
- 1 teaspoon paprika
- ½ cup blender grated Parmesan cheese

BARBECUE

Spicy Barbecue Sauce

Into container put

1 teaspoon dry mustard
1/3 cup vinegar
1 tablespoon Worcestershire sauce
1/4 cup chili sauce
1/4 cup brown sugar
1 teaspoon salt
1/4 teaspoon Tabasco
1 medium onion, coarsely cut

Cover and blend on high speed for 10 seconds, or until onion is finely chopped. Pour into a saucepan and simmer for 15 minutes. Use to baste meat or chicken during roasting. Makes about 1 1/4 cups.

Barbecue Sauce I

(For Spareribs, Pork Chops, Roast Pork, or Duckling)

Into container put

1/4 cup lemon juice
1/4 cup salad oil
1/2 teaspoon salt
1/4 teaspoon ginger
3/4 cup drained cooked apricots

Cover and blend on high speed for 30 seconds. Heat until bubbling. Makes 1 1/4 cups.

Barbecue Sauce II

(For Meat or Chicken)

Into container put

2 medium onions, quartered
1/4 cup salad oil
1 teaspoon dry mustard
1 tablespoon Worcestershire sauce

(see over)

¼ cup lemon juice
Strip yellow lemon rind
½ cup chili sauce
1 small hot chili pepper
¼ cup brown sugar
1 teaspoon salt
6 peppercorns

Cover and blend on high speed for 20 seconds. Pour into a saucepan and heat until bubbly. Makes 1½ cups.

Barbecue Sauce III

(For Meat or Chicken)

Into container put

1 medium onion, quartered
1 clove garlic
1 bottle (12 ounces) chili sauce
1 teaspoon orégano
1 teaspoon tarragon
Juice of 1 lemon
¼ cup salad oil
1 teaspoon salt
1 teaspoon dry mustard
3 dashes Tabasco
1 tablespoon Worcestershire sauce
2 to 4 tablespoons sugar
¼ cup red wine or water

Cover and blend on high speed for 10 seconds. Use cold for basting roasts or chops. For a cooked sauce, simmer in a saucepan for 30 minutes. Makes 3 cups.

SPAGHETTI

Sicilian Spaghetti Sauce

Into container put

2 cloves garlic
1 medium onion, coarsely cut

¼ teaspoon basil
¼ teaspoon celery salt
¼ teaspoon orégano
1 tablespoon parsley clusters
½ teaspoon salt
½ cup white wine, such as sauterne
½ pound mushrooms, cut in halves

Cover and blend on high speed for 15 seconds. Add

1 can (6 ounces) tomato paste
1 can (1 pound) tomatoes
5 olives, pitted
1 tablespoon capers
1 tablespoon raisins

Cover and blend on low speed for 15 seconds longer. Pour sauce into saucepan, bring to a boil, and simmer over low heat for 30 minutes, stirring occasionally. If desired, olives, capers, and raisins may be omitted. Makes 2 cups, or enough for 2 to 3 servings.

Red-Wine Spaghetti Sauce

Into container put

1 cup red wine
1 4-ounce can mushrooms or ½ pound fresh mushrooms
1 6-ounce can tomato paste
1 medium onion, coarsely cut
1 clove garlic
1 teaspoon salt
¼ teaspoon pepper
1 tablespoon sugar
½ teaspoon basil

Cover container and blend on high speed for 10 seconds. In a large skillet heat 2 tablespoons oil. Add 1 pound ground-beef chuck. Brown meat and add the mixture from container and 1 1-pound can tomatoes. Cover and simmer for 45 minutes. Remove lid and simmer for 15 minutes longer, in order to thicken sauce. Serve over spaghetti. Makes 4 cups, or enough for 4 to 6 servings.

Quick Spaghetti Sauce

In a large skillet heat 1 tablespoon olive oil. In it sauté, stirring until brown, ½ pound ground beef. Into container put

2 8-ounce cans tomato sauce
1 large onion, coarsely sliced
¼ cup parsley clusters
1 teaspoon salt
¼ teaspoon pepper
1 clove garlic
½ teaspoon orégano

Cover and turn motor on high. Remove cover and pour in

1½ cups water

Pour sauce over meat, bring to a boil, and simmer over low heat for 20 minutes, stirring occasionally. Serve over spaghetti with grated Parmesan cheese. Makes 4 cups, or enough for 4 to 6 servings.

MISCELLANEOUS

Avocado Sauce from Caracas

(For Almost Any Fried or Broiled Fish)

Into container put

1 large avocado, peeled and coarsely sliced
1 tablespoon vinegar
3 tablespoons olive oil
½ tablespoon lemon juice
½ teaspoon salt
¼ teaspoon black pepper

Cover container and blend on high speed for 20 seconds, or until consistency of mayonnaise, stopping to stir down if necessary. Makes about 1¼ cups.

Spicy Bahamian Sauce

(For Cooked Flounder, Halibut, Haddock, Sea Trout, or Snapper—or for Spaghetti)

Into container put

3 medium onions
1 green pepper, seeded and cut into strips

Add water just to cover, cover container, and blend on high speed for 2 to 3 seconds, or until vegetables are finely chopped. Drain and empty vegetables into a saucepan. Add

1 1-pound can tomatoes
½ teaspoon thyme
¼ teaspoon black pepper
¼ teaspoon cayenne
¼ cup water
1½ teaspoons salt

Bring to a boil and simmer for 30 minutes. Add more water if needed, to keep the sauce a medium-thick consistency. Serve hot or let cool and refrigerate in a pottery container. It is better the next day. To reheat, simmer for 10 minutes. Makes 4 cups.

Creole Sauce

(For Fish, Meat, or Vegetables)

Sauté for 5 minutes in ¼ cup butter, 1 medium onion, coarsely cut, and ½ green pepper, seeded and cut into strips. Transfer to container and add

1½ cups canned tomatoes
1 slice garlic clove
1 teaspoon salt
⅛ teaspoon pepper

Cover and blend for 3 seconds, or until vegetables are coarsely chopped. Heat and serve. Makes 2 cups.

Cumberland Sauce

(For Duck)

Into container put

2 wide strips orange rind of orange
½ cup currant jelly
¼ cup sherry or port
¼ cup orange juice
2 tablespoons lemon juice
1 teaspoon dry mustard
1 teaspoon cornstarch

Cover and blend on high speed for 10 seconds, or until rind is finely cut. Pour into a saucepan and simmer for 5 minutes, stirring occasionally. Makes 1 cup.

Curry Sauce

(For Cooked Lamb or Chicken)

Into container put

1 large onion, coarsely cut
1 clove garlic

Add water to cover, cover container, and blend on high speed for 3 to 4 seconds, or until vegetables are finely chopped. Drain. In a saucepan melt 2 tablespoons butter. In it sauté for 5 minutes the chopped, drained vegetables and 1 tablespoon curry powder, or to taste. Into container put

4 tablespoons flour
2 tablespoons butter
1 can hot beef consommé

Cover and blend on high speed for 20 seconds. Remove cover and, with motor on, pour in

1 cup hot water

Continue blending for 3 seconds. Add mixture to saucepan and cook over low heat for 10 minutes, stirring occasionally. Makes 2 cups.

Horse-Radish Sauce

(For Cooked Shrimp and Other Shellfish)

Into container put

¼ pound fresh horse-radish root, peeled and coarsely cut, or 2 tablespoons bottled horse-radish
½ cup chili sauce
½ cup vinegar
1 tablespoon Worcestershire sauce
½ teaspoon Tabasco
1 stalk celery with leaves, coarsely cut

1 small onion, halved
¼ teaspoon salt

Cover container and blend on high speed for 20 seconds, stopping to stir down if necessary. Chill. Makes 2 cups.

Horse-Radish-Cream Sauce

Into container put

½ cup heavy cream

Turn motor on high. Remove cover and stop motor the minute the cream begins to set around the blades. Add

¼ teaspoon salt
2 tablespoons horse-radish

Flick motor on and off 3 times. Serve with ham, tongue, or boiled beef. Makes 1 cup.

Pesto

(A Delicious Italian Sauce for Cooked Spaghetti)

Into container put

½ cup olive oil
¼ teaspoon basil
¼ cup parsley clusters
2 cloves garlic
½ teaspoon salt
½ cup walnuts
1 tablespoon blender-grated Parmesan cheese

Cover container and blend on high speed for 15 seconds. Makes ⅔ cup.

Classic Salsa Verde

(For Boiled Meats)

Into container put

1 cup parsley clusters
¼ cup capers, drained

(*see over*)

4 anchovy fillets
1 or 2 cloves garlic, to taste
1 thin slice medium onion
2 small sour gherkins
1 boiled potato the size of an egg, or 1 slice white bread soaked in water
¼ teaspoon salt
⅛ teaspoon pepper
½ cup olive oil
1 tablespoon wine vinegar

Cover container and blend on high speed for 15 seconds, stopping to stir down if necessary. Serve lukewarm. If preferred, onion, pickles, and vinegar may be omitted. Makes about 1 cup.

Chapter 9 PRESERVES

Vegetable relishes, catchups and chili sauces, fruit marmalades, and butters are simple to preserve when an electric blender does the chopping chore.

For real, honest, old-fashioned-flavor and goodness, homemade preserves can't be beat! And they are cheaper too. Small batches can be prepared in a twinkling within the limitations of the smallest city-apartment kitchen.

Nor is there any real reason to wait for the preserving season to roll around, nor for the facilities of a cold cellar room in which to store the finished jars. Cucumbers, onions, green peppers, beets, cauliflower and cabbages, frozen corn and string beans, apples, and, of course, citrus fruits for marmalades are available to us most of the year.

For example, you can make 8 pints of real homemade-flavored "out-of-season" mustard pickles in less than an hour at a cost of one half the price of a commercial brand, and without shedding an onion tear!

So, when you need a few jars of relish or marmalade, blender-make them and enjoy them. There are always more to be "custom-made" with an electric blender.

These few recipes were selected to show you the blender techniques in making preserves. From them you can easily adapt your favorite recipe from the long method to the new-fashioned blender way.

GOOSEBERRY
ORANGE
MARMALADE
PEACH
GRAPE
CURRANT
CRANBERRY

BUTTERS

Spicy Apple Butter

Into container put

1 pound green cooking apples, washed, cut into eighths and cored
½ cup water or apple juice
1 teaspoon cinnamon
1 cup sugar
¼ teaspoon allspice
½ teaspoon nutmeg
¼ teaspoon clove
⅛ teaspoon salt
1 ½-inch slice lemon

Cover and blend on high speed for 15 seconds. Pour into saucepan and cook over very low heat for 45 minutes, stirring occasionally. Pour boiling hot into small sterilized jars, and seal. Other fruits may be used in place of the apples, such as quince, hard pears, or plums. Makes about 1 pint.

JAMS

Apple Jam

Peel, cut into eighths and core 5 pounds apples. Fill container half full of apple slices and add ½ cup water. Cover container and blend on high speed for 15 seconds, or until fruit is the consistency of applesauce. Continue blending more fruit and water until all the fruit has been blended. Into a saucepan put

5 cups blender-made apple purée
1 teaspoon allspice
1½ teaspoons cinnamon
¼ cup lemon juice
7½ cups sugar

Mix well and bring to a full rolling boil over high heat. Boil for 1 minute, stirring constantly. Remove from heat. At once stir in ½ bottle fruit pectin. Skim off foam with wooden spoon. Then stir and skim for 5 minutes to cool slightly and prevent floating fruit.

Ladle into glasses and cover with a thin layer of hot paraffin. Makes about 12 medium glasses.

Apricot Jam

Soak ½ pound (about 1¾ cups) dried apricots in 3½ cups water for 4 hours, or overnight. Drain, reserving the liquid. Fill container half full of apricots and cover with water. Flick motor on and off high speed 3 times, or until fruit is chopped. Drain. Continue chopping fruit with water until all fruit has been used. Drain. Into a large saucepan put 4 cups chopped apricots, the reserved liquid, ¼ cup lemon juice, and 7 cups sugar. Mix well. Bring to a full rolling boil over high heat and boil hard for 1 minute, stirring constantly. Remove from heat. At once stir in ½ bottle fruit pectin. Skim off foam with wooden spoon. Then stir and skim for 5 minutes to cool slightly and prevent fruit from floating. Ladle into glasses. Cover at once with a thin layer of hot paraffin. Makes about 10 medium glasses.

Rhubarb Jam

Cut 2 pounds rhubarb into 2-inch pieces. Fill container three quarters' full of rhubarb and add water just to cover. Flick motor on and off high speed 2 or 3 times, until fruit has been chopped into small pieces. Drain and empty rhubarb into saucepan. Continue until all fruit has been chopped. Add ¼ cup lemon juice and ¾ cup water. Bring to a boil, cover, and simmer for about 1 minute, or until rhubarb is soft. Measure 3 cups rhubarb and juice into a large saucepan. Add 5½ cups sugar. Mix well. Bring to a full rolling boil over high heat and boil hard for 1 minute, stirring constantly. Remove from heat. At once stir in ½ bottle fruit pectin. Skim off foam with a wooden spoon. Then stir and skim for 5 minutes to cool jam slightly and prevent fruit from floating. Pour into glasses and cover at once with a thin layer of hot paraffin. Makes about 8 medium glasses.

JUICE

Tomato Juice

To get the benefit of both pulp and skin, stew tomatoes with celery leaves and onions until soft. Blend small portions at a time on high speed for 5 seconds. Strain out seeds and bottle.

CATCHUP

New-Fashioned Catchup with an Old-Fashioned Flavor

Seed 2 ripe sweet red peppers and 2 sweet green peppers and cut into strips. Peel and coarsely cut 4 onions. Fill container three quarters' full of the vegetables and add water just to cover. Cover and blend on high speed for 5 to 6 seconds, or until vegetables are finely chopped. Drain and empty vegetables into preserving kettle. Repeat until all vegetables are chopped. Remove stems and quarter 24 medium tomatoes (about 8 pounds). Fill container three quarters' full of tomatoes and add

½ cup white vinegar

Cover and blend on high speed for 5 seconds, or until tomatoes are finely chopped. Empty mixture into kettle. Repeat approximately 5 times, using ½ cup white vinegar each time, or a total of 3 cups white vinegar. Add to kettle

3 cups sugar
3 tablespoons salt
3 teaspoons dry mustard
½ teaspoon cayenne, or to taste
A spice bag containing 1½ teaspoons allspice, 1½ teaspoons cloves, and 1½ teaspoons broken stick cinnamon

Bring to a boil, then put into a slow oven (325°) and cook, uncovered, until volume is reduced to half. Remove spice bag and seal immediately in hot sterilized jars. Makes 5 pints.

MARMALADE

Orange Marmalade

Remove skin in strips from 6 large oranges and 3 lemons. Into container put

½ of the strips of fruit skin
1 cup water

Cover and blend on high speed for 10 seconds. Pour into a saucepan. Repeat using remaining fruit peel and 1 cup water. Add to saucepan ⅛ teaspoon soda. Bring mixture to a boil and simmer for 30 minutes. Scoop pulp and juice from oranges and lemons and add to saucepan. Add 2 quarts water and simmer for 1 hour, or until peel is tender. Add 7½ cups sugar. Bring to a full rolling boil and boil rapidly for 15 minutes, or until jellying point is reached. Let cool 10 minutes before bottling to prevent fruit rind from floating. Pour into jelly glasses and cover with a thin layer of hot paraffin. Makes about 5 pints.

PICKLES

Mustard Pickles

Coarsely cut 4 medium cucumbers with peel, 4 large onions, 4 green peppers. Fill container to top with cut vegetables and add water barely to cover. Cover container and blend on high speed for about 6 seconds, or until vegetables are finely chopped. Drain and empty into a large bowl. Repeat about 5 more times, until all vegetables are chopped. Sprinkle with ¼ cup salt. Prepare 4 pounds vegetables, such as tiny silver-skin onions, cauliflower flowerettes, small gherkins (when in season). Put vegetables in bowl, cover with water, and add ½ cup salt. Let vegetables stand overnight. The next day drain chopped vegetables and put into preserving kettle. Drain and dry whole vegetables and add to kettle. Add 2 cans pimientos, chopped, 2½ to 3 cups sugar to taste, 3 cups cider vinegar, and 1 tablespoon hot red-pepper flakes, or to taste. Bring mixture to a boil. Combine

¾ cup flour
¼ cup dry mustard
1½ tablespoons turmeric

1 tablespoon celery salt
1 cup cider vinegar

Stir the flour paste into the pickles and cook, stirring, for 10 minutes. Pack while hot into clean jars, and seal. Makes 10 pints.

RELISHES

Almond-Cranberry Relish

Into container put

¼ cup hot water
1 medium orange, peeled and seeded
1 strip orange rind
½ teaspoon ginger

Cover and blend on high speed for 5 seconds. Remove cover and add

2 cups fresh or frozen thawed cranberries
½ cup blanched almonds

Cover and blend on high speed for 15 seconds, stopping to stir down if necessary. Turn into saucepan and add 1¼ cups sugar and pinch salt. Cook over low heat for 15 minutes, stirring occasionally. Cool. Makes 2 cups.

Beet Relish

Fill container to within 2 inches of top with

Peeled, sliced raw beets

Add

2 tablespoons soft butter
1 tablespoon sugar
2 tablespoons cornstarch
¼ cup vinegar
1 teaspoon salt
1 cup water

Cover and blend on high speed for 6 seconds, or until last beet is drawn down into blades. Pour into saucepan and cook over low heat for 15 minutes, stirring occasionally, until beets are tender and juice is thickened. Chill and serve with roast beef. Makes about 2 cups.

Corn Relish

Prepare 1 cup coarsely cut onions, 3 cups coarsely diced sweet red pepper, and 4 cups coarsely sliced cabbage. Fill container three-quarters' full of vegetables and add water just to cover. Cover container and blend on high speed for about 6 seconds. Do not overblend. Drain and empty vegetables into a bowl. Continue until all vegetables have been chopped. In a large saucepan combine the chopped vegetables with 8 cups cut corn. Add

1 cup water
2 tablespoons dry mustard
1 tablespoon mustard seed
1 tablespoon celery seed
1 tablespoon salt
4 cups vinegar
1½ to 2 cups sugar
1 tablespoon turmeric

Mix well, bring to a boil, and simmer for 20 minutes. Pack while hot into hot jars and seal at once. Makes 4 pints.

Cucumber Relish

Prepare 8 cups coarsely cut cucumbers, 1 cup coarsely cut onions, and 2 cups seeded, sweet red pepper, cut into strips. Fill container three quarters' full of cut vegetables. Cover with water. Cover container and blend on high speed not more than 6 seconds. Drain and empty vegetables into a large bowl. Continue until all vegetables are chopped and drained. Sprinkle with 1 tablespoon turmeric. Add ½ cup salt dissolved in 2 quarts cold water. Let stand 3 to 4 hours. Drain. Cover again with cold water and let stand 1 hour. Drain. Tie in a bag 1 tablespoon mustard seed, 2 sticks cinnamon, 2 teaspoons cloves, and 2 teaspoons allspice. Put spices into a saucepan with 1½ cups brown sugar and 4 cups vinegar. Bring vinegar to a boil, pour over vegetables, and let stand overnight, or for 12 hours. The next day, bring vegetables and liquid to a boil. Pack into hot jars and seal at once. Makes 3 pints.

Green-Pepper Relish

Prepare 8 green peppers, seeded and sliced, and 3 large onions, coarsely cut. Fill container three quarters' full of peppers and onions and add water just to cover. Cover container and blend on high speed for not more than 6 seconds. Do not overblend. Drain and empty into a bowl. Continue until all vegetables are chopped. Cover vegetables with boiling water and let stand for 15 minutes. Drain, cover again with fresh boiling water, and let stand for 15 minutes. Drain and put vegetables into saucepan or kettle. Add ½ cup sugar, 1 tablespoon salt, and 1½ cups vinegar. Mix well, bring to a boil, and simmer for 30 minutes. Pack while hot into jars and seal at once. Makes 3 pints.

Hot-Pepper Relish

Into container put

- 2 green peppers, seeded and sliced
- 2 sweet red peppers, seeded and sliced
- 1 stalk celery, coarsely cut
- ½ large onion, coarsely cut
- ¾ teaspoon salt
- ¼ cup sugar
- ¼ cup vinegar
- ½ teaspoon hot-pepper flakes
- ⅛ teaspoon nutmeg
- ⅛ teaspoon cinnamon

Cover and blend on high speed for 4 seconds. Empty into a saucepan. Bring to a boil and simmer for 20 minutes. Cool and serve, or pack while hot into a hot jar and seal for future use. Makes 1 pint.

Red Relish

Prepare 4 cups coarsely cut cooked beets, 1 cup coarsely cut onions, 1 green pepper, seeded and cut into strips, and 4 cups coarsely sliced cabbage. Fill container three quarters' full of vegetables, and add water just to cover. Cover container and flick motor on and off high speed 2 or 3 times, or until vegetables are chopped into small pieces. Drain and empty vegetables into a bowl. Repeat until all vegetables are chopped. Put vegetables in a saucepan or kettle and add 1 tablespoon horse-radish, 1½ cups sugar (or to taste), 3 cups white vinegar, and 1 tablespoon salt. Bring to a boil and simmer for 10 minutes. Pack while hot into hot jars and seal at once. Makes 3 pints.

Tomato-Corn Relish

Into container put

- 1 cup coarsely cut onions
- 1 cup coarsely cut cucumber
- 1½ cups cut tomatoes
- 1 hot pepper
- ½ cup sugar
- 1 teaspoon salt
- ½ tablespoon mustard seed
- ½ tablespoon celery seed
- 1 teaspoon turmeric
- 1 cup vinegar

Cover container and blend on high speed for 4 seconds. Empty into a saucepan and add 1 package (10 ounces) frozen corn kernels. Bring to a boil and simmer for 30 minutes. Cool and serve, or pack into a hot jar and seal at once. Makes 1 pint.

Chapter 10 HOT BREADS

The highest popovers, the most tender pancakes and waffles are yours with an electric blender. Quick breads are made more quickly, and many new fruit-flavored breads are possible when fresh or dried fruits are puréed in an electric blender with the liquid ingredients.

In addition, the electric blender extends and speeds the action of yeast in the making of yeast bread and rolls, eliminating the need for kneading. Everyone who owns a blender can enjoy the wonderful aroma and flavor of homemade bread. The recipes for yeast breads that can be made in the electric blender are endless. The few included in this chapter are only samples. Once you have learned the technique of blending yeast batter, any one of your favorite recipes can be adapted to the blender method.

CORN, DATE, AND NUT MUFFINS

PANCAKES

Pancakes

Into container put

1 cup milk
1 cup pancake mix
1 egg
1 tablespoon melted shortening or cooking oil

Cover and blend just until flour is mixed in, about 8 seconds, stopping to stir down once. Pour out of container onto hot greased griddle ¼ cup at a time, and bake until brown on both sides. Makes 8.

Orange Pancakes

Into container put

1 cup orange juice
¼ cup milk
3 tablespoons melted butter or cooking oil
1 egg
3 tablespoons sugar
¾ teaspoon salt
1½ cups sifted flour
2½ teaspoons baking powder

Cover container and blend on high speed for 15 seconds, stopping to stir down once. Pour from container ¼ cup at a time onto a hot greased griddle and bake until cakes are browned on both sides. Serve with Orange Sauce. Makes 12 small pancakes. Serves 4.

Perfect Popovers

Into container put

1 cup milk
2 eggs
1 cup sifted flour
¼ teaspoon salt

Cover and blend on high speed for 15 seconds. Pour into greased and heated muffin pans or custard cups and bake in a preheated 425° F. oven for 40 minutes. Makes 8.

WAFFLES

Chocolate Waffles

Into mixing bowl sift 2 cups sifted flour and 3 teaspoons baking powder. Into container put

2 ounces unsweetened chocolate, cut into pieces
½ cup hot milk

Cover and blend on high speed for 20 seconds. Add

3 eggs
½ cup sugar
½ teaspoon salt
¼ cup melted butter
½ teaspoon vanilla

Cover and turn motor on high speed. Uncover and, with motor on, add

1 cup milk

Pour mixture over dry ingredients and mix lightly. Bake in hot waffle iron. Serve hot with whipped cream. Makes 8.

MUFFINS

Corn, Date, and Nut Muffins

Into container put

⅔ cup milk
1 egg

Cover and blend on high speed for 3 seconds. Add

1 package corn-muffin mix

Cover and blend on high speed for 12 seconds. Add

12 pitted dates
½ cup nut meats

Turn motor on high and push dates and nuts down into blades with a rubber spatula, being careful not to dip spatula too deeply. Continue to blend for 15 seconds. Spoon batter into greased muffin cups and bake in a preheated 400° F. oven for 20 minutes. Makes 12.

Cranberry-Orange Muffins

Into mixing bowl sift 2 cups sifted flour and 3 teaspoons baking powder. Into container put

1 cup fresh or defrosted cranberries
1 cup milk
Thin yellow rind of 1 orange
1 egg
3 tablespoons soft butter or shortening
⅔ cup sugar
½ teaspoon salt

Cover and blend on high speed until cranberries are finely chopped. Pour over dry ingredients and stir just to moisten flour. Turn into greased muffin cups and bake in a preheated 400° F. oven for 25 minutes. Makes 1½ dozen medium muffins.

BREADS

Banana Tea Loaf

Sift into a mixing bowl 1¾ cups sifted flour, ¾ teaspoon baking soda, 1¼ teaspoons cream of tartar, and ½ teaspoon salt. Into container put

2 eggs
½ cup soft butter or shortening
2 small ripe bananas, sliced
¾ cup sugar

Cover and blend on high speed for 20 seconds. Pour over dry ingredients and mix just to combine. Turn into a greased loaf pan and bake in a preheated 350° F. oven for about 45 minutes. Makes 1 loaf 8 x 4 inches.

Orange-Date Loaf

Into mixing bowl sift 2 cups sifted flour, 1½ teaspoons baking powder, and ½ teaspoon baking soda. Into container put

½ cup hot water
⅔ cup dates

Cover and turn motor on high, remove cover and, with motor on, drop in, piece by piece,

1 orange, cut in quarters and seeded

Add

1 egg

2 tablespoons soft butter or shortening

½ teaspoon salt

¾ cup sugar

Continue to blend for 20 seconds; then add

½ cup nut meats

Turn off motor as soon as last nut is drawn down into blades. Pour mixture over dry ingredients and mix lightly. Turn into greased 9½ x 5½-inch loaf pan and bake in a preheated 350° F. oven for 55 to 60 minutes.

Dilly Bread

Into container put

1 package dry yeast

¼ cup warm water

Let stand for 5 minutes; then cover and blend on high speed for 20 seconds. Add

1 cup creamy-style cottage cheese

1 tablespoon dehydrated minced onion

1 tablespoon liquid shortening

1 teaspoon salt

¼ teaspoon baking soda

1 egg

2 tablespoons dill weed

Cover and blend on high speed for 20 seconds. Measure into a bowl 2¼ cups flour. Pour blended mixture over flour and mix with spoon, adding if necessary about ½ cup more flour to make a stiff dough that pulls away from side of bowl. Pick up dough with floured hands and pat into a ball. Return to bowl, cover, and let rise until double in bulk. Put into a greased pan 8½ x 4½ x 2¾. Let rise until double in bulk; then bake in a preheated 350° F. oven for 40 to 50 minutes.

Potato Bread

Into container put

1 package dry yeast
½ cup lukewarm potato water

Let stand for 5 minutes, then cover and blend on high speed for 20 seconds. Add

⅓ cup shortening
1 cup lukewarm milk
1 egg
1½ teaspoons salt
1 cup cooked, drained potatoes

Cover and turn motor on low speed. Switch to high speed and blend for 20 seconds. Measure into a bowl 4 cups flour. Pour blended mixture over flour and stir with spoon, adding if necessary from ¼ to ½ cup more flour to make a dough that pulls away from the sides of the bowl. Pick up dough with floured hands and pat into a firm ball. Return dough to bowl, cover and let rise for 2½ hours, or until double in bulk. Form dough into a ball and press gently into a greased 8-inch cake pan. Cover and let rise. Bake in a 375° F. oven for about 45 minutes.

Rice Bread

Into container put

1 envelope dry yeast
½ cup lukewarm water
1 teaspoon salt

Let stand for 5 minutes, then cover and blend on high speed for 20 seconds. Add

1½ cups warm milk
3 teaspoons sugar
1 cup cooked rice

Cover and blend on high speed for 10 seconds. Pour into mixing bowl over 4½ cups flour. Stir with spoon until well mixed. Gather up dough with floured hands and shape into a loaf to fit a well-greased loaf pan, 10 x 6¼ x 2½. Let rise until double in bulk. Brush with beaten egg and bake in a 375° F. oven for 50 to 60 minutes, or until browned. Cool on rack. This bread is particularly good sliced and toasted. Serve very fresh, or reheat before serving.

Sweet-Potato Bread

Into container put

- 1 envelope dry yeast
- ½ cup lukewarm water
- 1 teaspoon salt

Let stand for 5 minutes, then cover and blend on high speed for 20 seconds. Add

- ¾ cup milk, scalded with 3 tablespoons butter and cooled to lukewarm
- 1 cup sweet potatoes

Cover and blend on high speed for 10 seconds. Pour mixture into a large bowl over 3½ cups flour and ½ cup sugar. Stir until well mixed. Cover and let rise until double in bulk. Flour hands, gather up dough, and form into a ball. Shape to fit into a greased loaf pan, 9¼ x 5¼ x 2½. Let rise until double in bulk and bake in a preheated 375° F. oven for 45 minutes, or until lightly browned. Remove from oven and brush with butter while still hot. Cool on rack.

ROLLS

Basic Rolls

Into container put

- 1 package dry yeast
- 1 cup lukewarm water

Let stand for 5 minutes; then cover and blend on high speed for 20 seconds. Add

- ¼ cup liquid shortening
- 1 egg
- 1 teaspoon salt

Cover and blend on high speed for 3 seconds. Pour into bowl over 3 cups flour. Stir until thoroughly mixed. Cover and let rise for 1½ hours, or until double in bulk. Stir down. Fill greased muffin tins half full of dough and let rise about 45 minutes, or until double in bulk. Brush with beaten egg yolk and bake in a preheated 375° F. oven for 25 minutes. Makes 2 dozen. If desired, top rolls with poppy or sesame seeds, or with a mixture of butter, brown sugar, and chopped nuts.

NOTE: For a softer top on the rolls, brush with melted butter while still hot from the oven.

Four Flavors from Basic-Roll Recipe

After basic dough in recipe above has risen, punch down and divide into 4 parts. Put each part in a bowl and add and mix one of the following ingredients into each part. Fill greased muffin tins half full of dough and let rise about 45 minutes, or until double in bulk. Bake in a preheated 375° F. oven for 25 minutes. Makes 6 rolls each of 4 different flavors.

1. ¼ cup drained crushed pineapple
2. ¼ cup raisins, blended for 5 seconds
3. ¼ cup blender-chopped walnuts mixed with 2 teaspoons cinnamon and 2 teaspoons sugar
4. ¼ cup blender-grated Cheddar cheese

Chapter 11 CAKES, COOKIES, FILLINGS, AND FROSTINGS

The electric blender is *not* a beater. It is exactly what it is called—a blender; and when it comes to the making of those high, fluffy, tender cakes so popular in American cuisine, no appliance can surpass the old-fashioned method of hand-creaming the butter and sugar, and beating in the milk alternately with the dry ingredients.

We call it the old-fashioned method—and rightly so, for today, de luxe cake mixes are rapidly taking the place of homemade cake batters. Few women can top them for consistency of texture and flavor.

There are some types of cakes, however—rich, moist, and fruit-filled—that the blender can produce most efficiently, and it plays an important role in the blending of cake toppings, fillings, and frostings. The following recipe for Chocolate Butter Cream, once again dramatically illustrates how the electric blender effortlessly makes recipes often considered too difficult or too time-consuming for the average homemaker. Try flavoring it with a generous dollop of dark rum instead of vanilla! It will make any cake taste as if it came right out of a Viennese pastryshop!

Chocolate Butter Cream

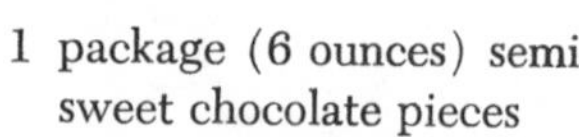

1 package (6 ounces) semi-sweet chocolate pieces
¼ cup boiling water
4 egg yolks
1 teaspoon vanilla
1 stick soft butter

Empty package of chocolate bits into blender container. Add boiling water, cover, and blend on high speed for 20 seconds.

Turn off motor. Add egg yolks and vanilla. Cover and turn motor on high speed.

With motor on, uncover and drop in butter. If butter is too hard, a vortex may cease to form. Break surface of mixture with a rubber spatula, being careful not to dip too deeply. Blend for 15 seconds, or until frosting is smooth. If frosting is too soft, chill in refrigerator until of spreading consistency.

For a really French Chocolate Butter Cream, omit the vanilla and flavor the frosting to taste with cognac or dark rum. Makes sufficient creamy chocolate frosting to fill and frost an 8-inch cake or 12 cupcakes.

Quick Dobosch Torte

Slice a bakery poundcake, round or oblong, into 6 thin layers with a serrated knife. This can be done very easily if the cake is thoroughly chilled or frozen before cutting. Put the layers together with Chocolate Butter Cream between and frost top and sides of cake. Store cake in refrigerator, where it will remain fresh for many days.

Fluffy Yellow Cake with Marshmallow Topping

Sift into mixing bowl 2¼ cups sifted flour, ¼ teaspoon salt, and 2½ teaspoons baking powder. Into container put

½ cup shortening or soft butter
1½ cups sugar
2 eggs
1 teaspoon vanilla

Cover and blend on high speed for 15 seconds. Uncover and, with motor on, gradually add 1 cup milk. Pour milk mixture over dry ingredients and stir to combine thoroughly. Spoon batter into a greased 8 x 12-inch baking pan. Arrange marshmallows over batter, keeping them 1 inch from sides of pan. Sprinkle marshmallows with a mixture of ½ cup blender-chopped pecans and ½ cup brown sugar. Bake in a preheated 350° F. oven for 40 minutes, or until cake tests done. Cool and serve from the pan.

Applesauce Cake with Macaroon Topping

Sift into a mixing bowl 2 cups sifted flour, 1 teaspoon cinnamon, ½ teaspoon cloves, 2 teaspoons baking soda, and ¼ teaspoon salt. Into container put

½ cup shortening or soft butter
1 cup brown sugar
1 egg
1 teaspoon vanilla
1½ cups applesauce

Cover and blend on high speed for 30 seconds. Turn off motor and add

1 cup walnuts

Stir to combine, cover, and blend on high speed for 15 seconds. Combine with the dry ingredients. Turn into a greased 8-inch-square pan and bake in a preheated 350° F. oven for 40 minutes. Into container put

2 egg whites
1 cup confectioners' sugar

Cover and blend on high speed for 8 seconds. Add

1 teaspoon vanilla
1 can (3½ ounces) shredded coconut

Cover and blend for 15 seconds longer. Spread on hot cake and brown under broiler heat for 3 to 4 minutes.

Date Cake with Pecan Topping

Sift 1½ cups sifted flour into mixing bowl. Into container put

1 cup halved, pitted dates
1 cup boiling water
1 teaspoon baking soda

Cover and blend on high speed for 15 seconds. Add

½ cup soft butter
1 cup sugar
1 egg
½ teaspoon salt
1 teaspoon vanilla

Cover and blend on high speed for 20 seconds. Combine with dry ingredients.

Pour into greased 8-inch-square pan and bake in a preheated 350° F. oven for 40 minutes, or until cake tests done. While cake is baking put into container

1 cup pecan meats
½ cup brown sugar
4 tablespoons melted butter
2 tablespoons milk

Cover and blend on high speed for 10 seconds. Spread on top of cake and place under broiler heat for 3 to 4 minutes, or until browned. Let cake cool in pan.

Nut-Filled Devil's Food

Into container put

⅔ cup shortening or soft butter
1¾ cups sugar
2 eggs
2 egg yolks
½ cup cocoa
½ cup warm water

Cover and blend on high speed for 30 seconds. Add

½ cup walnuts
1 cup coconut

Cover and blend on high speed for 10 seconds. Pour mixture into a bowl and gradually stir in ¾ cup sour milk alternately with a mixture of 2¼ cups sifted flour, 1 teaspoon baking soda, and ½ teaspoon salt. Turn into a greased 9-inch-square pan and bake in a preheated 350° F. oven for 50 minutes. Serve warm with whipped cream.

Cracker Cake

Blender-grate 1 cup nut meats and empty into mixing bowl. Blender-crumb 27 graham crackers, 6 at a time, to make 2 cups crumbs, and empty into bowl with the nuts. Stir in 2 tablespoons flour, ¼ teaspoon salt and 2 teaspoons baking powder. Into container put

½ cup shortening or soft butter
1 cup sugar
3 eggs

Cover and blend on low speed for 20 seconds. With motor on, gradually add

¾ cup milk

Pour into dry ingredients and stir until mixed. Pour into two 8-inch greased layer-cake pans and bake in a preheated 350° F. oven for 30 minutes. Let cool for 10 minutes, then turn out on rack. When thoroughly cool, put together and frost with whipped cream or your favorite frosting.

Unbaked Fruitcake

Blender-grate ½ cup nut meats and empty into mixing bowl. Blender-crumb 24 graham crackers, 6 at a time, and empty crumbs into bowl. Into container put, in order listed,

6 graham crackers
½ cup sliced, pitted dates
½ cup coarsely cut dried apricots

Cover and blend on high speed for 16 seconds. Empty into bowl. Into container put

¼ cup soft butter
¼ cup confectioners' sugar
2 tablespoons corn syrup
½ cup orange marmalade
½ teaspoon cinnamon

½ teaspoon salt
⅛ teaspoon cloves

Cover and blend on high speed for 30 seconds, stopping to stir down if necessary. Add mixture to the crumb-nut mixture. Stir in ½ cup raisins, ¼ cup diced candied citron, and ¼ cup quartered candied cherries. Mix thoroughly. Add 2 tablespoons rum. Pack into a 3-cup mold and refrigerate for 48 hours before serving.

Pot-Cheesecake

Line a 6-cup loaf pan with crumbs (see Index for Crumb Crust). Into container put

3 eggs yolks
¾ cup sugar
¼ cup flour
½ teaspoon salt
½ cup heavy cream
Thinly shaved yellow rind from ½ lemon
1 tablespoon lemon juice

Cover and blend on high speed. Uncover and, with motor on, gradually add

12 ounces pot cheese (1½ cups)
1 8-ounce package soft cream cheese

When mixture is smooth, turn off motor. Beat 3 egg whites until stiff. Pour cheese mixture over egg whites and fold gently together until combined. Turn into lined loaf pan. Bake in a preheated 325° F. oven for 1 hour. Turn off oven and let cheesecake remain in oven for 30 minutes longer.

Sour-Cream Cheesecake

Line a 5-cup pan or mold with crumbs (see Index for Crumb Crust). Into container put

2 eggs
½ cup sugar
2 teaspoons vanilla
1½ cups sour cream

CHEESE CAKES

Cover and blend on high speed for 15 seconds. With motor on, gradually add

1 pound (2 8-ounce packages) soft cream cheese
2 tablespoons melted butter

Pour into prepared pan and bake in a preheated 325° F. oven for 30 to 40 minutes, or until set in center. The filling will be still very soft, but it will firm up as the cake cools. Chill thoroughly before serving.

Coconut Macaroons

Into container put

2 egg whites
1 cup confectioners' sugar

Cover and blend on high speed for 8 seconds. Add

1 teaspoon vanilla
1 can (3½ ounces) moist coconut

Cover and blend on high speed for 15 seconds. Drop batter from a teaspoon on baking sheet lined with aluminum foil and bake in a preheated 350° F. oven for 20 minutes. Remove cookies while still warm, using a steel spatula, to a cake rack to cool. Makes 16 small macaroons.

Hazelnut Cookies

Blender chop 2 cups hazelnuts (or pecans), 1 cup at a time. Set aside on piece of waxed paper. Into container put

3 eggs
½ cup sugar
1 teaspoon vanilla

Cover and blend on high speed for 30 seconds. Add

1 tablespoon bread crumbs
The nuts

Blend on low speed for 10 seconds, stopping to stir down if necessary. Drop from a teaspoon onto a greased baking sheet and bake in a preheated 300° F. oven for 15 minutes. Makes about 3 dozen.

FROSTINGS

Butterscotch Frosting

Into container put

2 tablespoons hot water
¼ cup soft butter
1 teaspoon vanilla
1 tablespoon dark corn syrup

Cover and blend on high speed for 5 seconds. Add

1 cup firmly packed dark brown sugar

Cover and blend on high speed for 10 seconds. Add

1 tablespoon hot water

Cover and blend on high speed until smooth. Add

1½ cups confectioners' sugar

Cover and blend on high speed for 10 seconds, or until smooth, stopping to stir down. Makes 1¼ cups. Sufficient frosting for 2 8- or 9-inch layers.

Chocolate-Mint Frosting

Into container put

1 cup sugar
¾ cup evaporated milk
4 squares bitter chocolate, cut into chunks
½ teaspoon mint flavoring

Cover and blend on high speed for 3 to 4 minutes, or until frosting becomes thick. And it *will* thicken! Makes 1½ cups, or enough for an 8- or 9-inch layer cake.

Creamy Vanilla Frosting

Into container put

1 egg white
1 teaspoon vanilla
¼ teaspoon salt
1 cup confectioners' sugar

Cover and blend on high speed for 5 seconds, or until smooth. Add

¼ cup soft butter
1 cup confectioners' sugar

Cover and blend on high speed for 10 seconds, or until smooth, stopping to stir down. Makes sufficient frosting for 1 9-inch layer. Makes 1 cup.

Fondant Frosting

Into measuring cup put 1 egg white, 2 teaspoons lemon juice, and water to measure a total of ⅓ cup liquid. Into container pour

The egg mixture

Turn motor on high, and gradually add

3 cups confectioners' sugar

Continue blending until mixture is smooth, stopping to stir down if necessary. This makes a stiff fondant-type frosting, sufficient to frost 2 8- or 9-inch layers. Makes about 1¼ cups.

Mocha Frosting

Into container put

⅓ cup hot coffee
½ cup soft butter
½ teaspoon vanilla

Cover and blend on high speed for 10 seconds, or until creamy. Add

¼ cup cocoa
2 cups confectioners' sugar

Cover and blend on high speed for 10 seconds. Add

1 cup confectioners' sugar

Cover and blend on high speed for 10 seconds longer, stopping to stir down if necessary. Makes about 1⅔ cups, or sufficient to frost 2 8- or 9-inch layers.

Orange-Walnut Butter Cream

Into container put

½ cup walnuts
Thinly sliced yellow rind of ½ orange

Cover and blend on high speed for 6 seconds, or until nuts are finely chopped. Add

5 tablespoons concentrated defrosted orange juice

(*see over*)

½ cup (1 stick) soft butter
2 cups confectioners' sugar

Stir to combine. Cover and blend on high speed for 30 seconds, stopping to stir down once or twice. Makes enough to frost 2 9-inch layers.

Raisin-Rum Frosting

Into container put

2 tablespoons heavy cream
3 tablespoons dark rum
½ cup seedless raisins

Cover and blend on high speed for 30 seconds. Add

½ cup (1 stick) soft butter
1½ cups confectioners' sugar

Cover and blend on high speed until frosting is smooth, stopping to stir down once or twice. Makes enough to frost 2 8-inch layers.

FILLINGS

Apricot-Date Filling

Cover ½ cup pitted dried prunes, ½ cup dried apricots, and ½ cup white raisins with boiling water and let stand for 30 minutes. Drain and empty fruit into container. Add

½ cup crushed pineapple with juice
2 thin strips yellow peel of 1 orange

Cover and turn motor on high speed. Uncover and stir surface of mixture with a rubber spatula to aid blending and allow fruit at top to be drawn down into blades. Turn off motor. Add

¼ cup walnut meats

Stir to combine, cover, and blend just long enough to crush the nuts. Makes 1 pint.

APRICOT-DATE-GINGER FILLING

Add 2 slices preserved ginger along with the pineapple.

NOTE: This makes an excellent tea-sandwich filling as well as a quick preserve to serve with roast turkey or pork. Recipe may be doubled to make 1 quart if desired.

Sour-Cream-Nut Filling

Into container put

- 1 cup nuts
- ½ cup raisins

Cover and blend on high speed for 10 seconds. Add

- ½ cup sour cream
- 4 tablespoons soft butter
- 1 cup confectioners' sugar

Cover and blend on high speed for 30 seconds, stopping to stir down once or twice. Makes 2 cups.

ORANGE PEACH PUDDING

Chapter 12 DESSERTS AND DESSERT SAUCES

If you have glanced through a few chapters in this book or have tried some of the exciting dishes, you will know by now that the electric blender can save many precious moments in the making of dishes from soups to—you guessed it—desserts.

But in addition to the usual timesaving chores of grinding nuts and puréeing fruits, the electric blender has become revolutionary in the dessert field. Only the electric blender, and no other electric appliance, can perform dessert tricks that are close to wizardry. A short time ago it was discovered that, by adding crushed ice to a gelatin mixture while it was blending, one could make frothy fruit-flavored desserts, rich Bavarian creams, and fluffy chiffon-pie fillings, ready to serve in less than two minutes! Try some for yourself and discover the magic of the electric blender.

Cheese Pie in Crumb Crust

16 graham-cracker squares
½ cup sugar
½ teaspoon cinnamon
¼ cup melted butter

Break 5 graham crackers at a time into blender container. Cover and blend on high speed for 5 seconds.

Empty crumbs into bowl. Repeat until all crackers are crumbed.

Add sugar, cinnamon, and melted butter. Stir until crumbs are moistened and press into a buttered 8-inch pie plate.

2 envelopes plain gelatin
Thin strips lemon peel
½ lemon
½ cup hot milk
¼ cup sugar
2 eggs
8 ounces cream cheese
1 cup cracked ice
1 cup cream

Empty gelatin into container. Add lemon peel, juice from the ½ lemon, and the hot milk. Cover and blend on high speed for 40 seconds.

Turn off motor. Add sugar, eggs, and cheese. Cover and blend on high speed for 10 seconds. Remove cover and, with motor on, add ice.

Pour in cream to bring liquid to top of container.

Turn off motor and quickly pour filling into prepared crust.

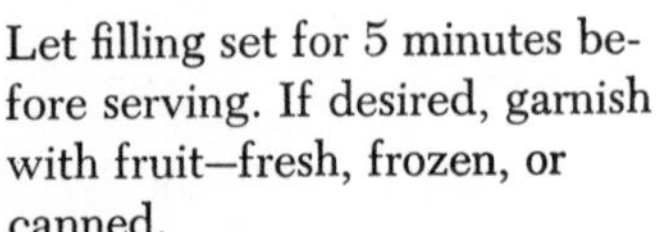

Let filling set for 5 minutes before serving. If desired, garnish with fruit—fresh, frozen, or canned.

QUICK SET

Charlotte Russe

Into container put

1 package strawberry-flavored gelatin
½ cup hot orange juice

Cover and blend on high speed for 15 seconds. Remove cover and, with motor on, add

1 heaping cup crushed ice
1 cup heavy cream

Continue to blend for 20 seconds longer. Pour into 4 individual dessert dishes and let set for 3 to 4 minutes. Top each with half a ladyfinger and sprinkle with confectioners' sugar. Chill. Serves 4.

Chocolate Bavarian Cream

Into container put

2 envelopes plain gelatin
¼ cup cold water
½ cup hot milk or strong coffee

Cover and blend on high speed for 40 seconds. Add

1 package (6 ounces) semisweet chocolate

Cover and blend on high speed for 10 seconds. Remove cover and, with motor on, add

2 egg yolks
1 cup cream
1 heaping cup crushed ice, or enough to bring liquid to top of container

Continue to blend for 20 seconds longer, then pour into 1 large 4-cup mold or into small individual molds. Serve with whipped cream. Serves 6.

Lime or Orange Divine

Into container put

⅔ cup hot water
2 envelopes plain gelatin

Cover and blend on high speed for 40 seconds. Add

½ cup sugar

Cover and blend on high speed for 2 seconds to dissolve sugar. Add

6 ounces partially defrosted fruit-ade

Cover and turn motor on high speed. Uncover and add

About 2 cups crushed ice, or enough to bring liquid to the top of container

Continue to blend for about 20 seconds. Turn off motor and spoon dessert into serving glasses. Serves 6.

Maple Chiffon Pie

Prepare a 9-inch baked pie shell or Crumb Crust. Into container put

¼ cup water
2 envelopes plain gelatin
¾ cup hot milk
1 teaspoon maple flavoring
Dash salt

Cover and blend on high speed for 40 seconds. Add

⅓ cup sugar

Cover and blend for 2 seconds. Add

½ cup heavy cream
1 teaspoon vanilla
2 cups crushed ice, or enough to bring liquid to top of container

Continue to blend for 30 seconds longer. Fold in ½ cup chopped nuts. Pour into pie shell and spread with whipped cream. Serves 6.

Sea Foam

Into container put

1 package lime-flavored gelatin
½ cup hot canned pineapple juice

Cover and blend on high speed for 20 seconds. Add

2 cups crushed ice

Cover and blend on high speed for 30 seconds. Pour into a 2-cup mold and chill until firm. Serves 4.

Six-Minute Jello

Into container put

1 package fruit-flavored gelatin
½ cup boiling water

Cover and blend on high speed for 6 seconds. Add

1½ heaping cups crushed ice

Cover and blend for 30 seconds. Pour into a 2-cup ring mold and chill for 5 minutes. Serves 4.

Strawberry Bavarian Cream

Defrost 1 package (10 ounces) frozen strawberries. Drain ½ cup juice into a saucepan and heat just to the simmering point. Into container put

2 envelopes plain gelatin
¼ cup cold milk
The hot strawberry juice

Cover and blend on high speed for 40 seconds. Add

¼ cup sugar
The defrosted strawberries
2 egg yolks

Cover and blend on high speed for 5 seconds. Remove cover and, with motor on, add

1 cup cream
1 heaping cup crushed ice, or enough to bring liquid to top of container

Continue to blend for 30 seconds longer, and pour into a 4-cup mold. Serves 6.

Strawberry Meringue

With a heavy knife cut 1 package (10 ounces) frozen strawberries into 16 pieces. Into container put

1 envelope plain gelatin
2 tablespoons lemon juice
½ cup boiling water

Cover and blend on high speed for 40 seconds. Add

2 egg whites

Cover and blend on high speed for 10 seconds. Remove cover and, with motor on, gradually drop in the pieces of frozen fruit, a few at a time. When all the fruit has been added and the mixture is smooth, spoon into serving glasses. Serves 4.

NOTE: For a creamy meringue, use 1 whole egg instead of 2 egg whites.

Vanilla Bavarian Cream

Into container put

2 envelopes plain gelatin
2 tablespoons water
1 tablespoon vanilla
½ cup hot milk

Cover and blend on high speed for 40 seconds. Add

¼ cup sugar
2 egg yolks

Cover and blend on high speed for 5 seconds. Remove cover and, with motor on, add

1 cup heavy cream
1 heaping cup crushed ice, or enough to bring liquid to top of container

Continue to blend for 20 seconds; then pour into a 4-cup mold. Serves 6.

CHILL AND SERVE

Blancmange with Raspberry Sauce

Into container put

3 cups milk
1 tablespoon soft butter
¼ teaspoon cinnamon

1 thin strip yellow lemon peel
¼ cup cornstarch
¼ cup sugar
¼ teaspoon salt

Cover and blend on high speed for 10 seconds. Remove cover and, with motor on add

⅓ cup blanched almonds

Turn off motor immediately. Pour into saucepan and cook over medium heat until thickened, stirring frequently. Add ½ teaspoon vanilla. Pour into 6 5-ounce individual molds, rinsed in cold water, and chill until firm, about 1½ hours. Unmold and serve with Raspberry Sauce. Serves 6.

Raspberry Sauce

Into container put

1 10-ounce package partially defrosted raspberries

Cover and blend on high speed for 15 seconds. Strain into sauceboat.

Fruit Velvet

Drain 1 1-pound can mixed fruit cocktail, reserving syrup. Heat ¼ cup of the syrup. Into container put

The hot syrup
1 envelope plain gelatin

Cover and blend on high speed for 40 seconds. Add

The fruit
The remaining syrup
1 tablespoon sherry

Cover and blend on high speed for 30 seconds. Remove cover and, with motor on, pour in ½ cup heavy cream. Pour into 4 individual serving dishes and chill until firm. Decorate with whipped cream. Serves 4.

Key-Lime Pie

Into container put

1 package lime-flavored gelatin
½ cup hot water
1 thin strip green rind of a lime

Cover and blend on high speed for 20 seconds. Add

½ cup lime juice
2 egg yolks

Cover and blend on high speed. Uncover and pour in

1⅓ cups (1 can) sweetened condensed milk
Few drops green food coloring

Pour blended mixture over 2 egg whites, stiffly beaten. Fold until combined. Turn into baked 9-inch pie shell and chill until firm. Serves 6.

Orange Bavarian Cream

Into container put

1 package orange-flavored gelatin
½ cup boiling water

Cover and blend on high speed for 20 seconds. Add

¾ cup crushed ice

Cover and blend on high speed for 30 seconds, or until ice is blended. Uncover and, with motor on, pour in

1 cup heavy cream

Pour into a 2-cup mold and chill until firm (about 30 minutes). Serves 4.

Orange Cream

Into container put

1 package orange-flavored gelatin
1 cup hot water

Cover and blend on high speed for 10 seconds. Add

8 ounces cream cheese, quartered
½ cup orange juice
2 tablespoons lemon juice
1 strip yellow rind from 1 orange

Cover and blend on high speed for 20 seconds. Pour into 4 individual molds and chill until firm. Unmold and serve with a raspberry purée. Serves 4.

Orange- or Apricot-Chiffon Pie

In a large mixing bowl beat 2 egg whites until stiff. Beat in 2 tablespoons sugar. Set egg whites aside. Into container put

2 envelopes plain gelatin
½ cup defrosted orange concentrate or apricot nectar
½ cup hot milk

Cover and blend on high speed for 40 seconds. Add

¼ cup sugar
2 egg yolks

Cover and blend for 5 seconds. Remove cover and pour in

1 cup heavy cream

With motor on, immediately add

1 heaping cup cracked or crushed ice

Blend for about 20 seconds, pour mixture over egg whites, and fold gently until mixed. Pile into an 8-inch crumb crust or baked pie shell and chill until ready to serve. Serves 6.

Orange Mousse

Into container put

2 envelopes plain gelatin
1 cup hot orange juice

Cover and blend on high speed for 40 seconds. Add

3 eggs
2 egg yolks
Thinly sliced yellow rind of ¼ orange
3 tablespoons sugar

Cover and blend on high speed for 5 seconds. Remove cover and, with motor on, add

1 heaping cup crushed ice

Continue to blend for 10 seconds. Pour into 4-cup mold and chill until set. Serves 6.

Orange-Peach Pudding

Into container put

1 envelope plain gelatin
½ cup hot milk

Cover and blend on high speed for 40 seconds. Add

2 eggs
½ cup cold milk
¼ cup sugar
Pinch salt
1 cup orange juice
1 strip thin yellow rind of a lemon
3 fresh peaches, peeled, pitted, and cut into quarters

Cover and blend on high speed for 20 seconds, or until smooth. Chill for 30 minutes; then fold in 1 cup heavy cream, whipped. Spoon into individual sherbet glasses and, if desired, top with additional fresh peach slices. Serves 4.

To Use Frozen Peaches: substitute a 10-ounce package frozen peaches, partially defrosted, for the fresh peaches and the sugar.

Pineapple Cream in Jelly

Into container put

1 package pineapple-flavored gelatin
¾ cup hot water

Cover and blend on high speed for 15 seconds. Remove cover and, with motor on, pour in

1 cup cold water

Pour a layer of the gelatin ¼ inch thick into a 8-cup dessert mold and chill until set. Garnish layer with drained canned pineapple slices and maraschino cherries. Cover fruit with a thin layer of gelatin, chill until set; then pour in remaining gelatin and chill until set. Into container put

1 package pineapple-flavored gelatin
½ cup hot water

Cover and blend on high speed for 15 seconds. Add

3 eggs
Pinch salt

Cover and turn motor on high. Remove cover and, with motor on, add

1 heaping cup crushed ice

Blend for 10 seconds longer. Fold in

1 cup heavy cream, whipped

Pour into mold over gelatin and fruit and chill until set. Unmold on cold serving platter and garnish with halved pineapple slices, cherries, and sprigs of fresh mint. Serves 8.

BLEND AND COOK

Lemon Meringue Pie

Into container put

¾ cup sugar
¼ cup cornstarch
Dash salt
1 cup water
¼ cup lemon juice
Yellow rind of 1 lemon
3 egg yolks
1 tablespoon butter

Cover and blend on high speed for 20 seconds. Turn into a saucepan and cook over low heat, stirring constantly, until thickened and smooth. Pour into a 9-inch baked pie shell.

Beat 3 egg whites until foamy and gradually add ⅓ cup sugar, about 1 tablespoon at a time. Continue beating until stiff and glossy. Spread over lemon filling in pie shell. Bake in a preheated 375° F. oven for 12 minutes. Serves 6.

Velvety Lemon Tartlets

Into container put

Yellow rind from 1 lemon
Juice of 1 lemon
3 eggs
¼ cup soft butter
¾ cup sugar
Dash salt

Cover and blend on high speed for 15 seconds. Turn into a double saucepan and cook over simmering water, until thickened, stirring occasionally. Turn into 8 baked tart shells (about 3 inches in diameter). Cool. Serves 8.

WHIPS

Apricot Whip

Into small saucepan put 1½ cups dried apricots, 1 cup water, ½ cup sugar, and 1 thin strip yellow lemon peel. Bring to a boil. Cover and simmer for 20 minutes. Cool. Empty apricots and juice into container. Cover and blend on high speed for 20 seconds, or until smooth. Fold into 1 cup heavy cream, whipped. Spoon into sherbet glasses and chill. Serves 6.

Date Whip

Simmer 8 ounces pitted dates and ½ cup orange juice for 10 minutes. Empty dates and juice into container, cover, and blend for 30 seconds. Add

1 teaspoon lemon juice
4 ounces pecan or walnut meats

Cover and blend for 10 seconds, or until nuts are finely chopped. Serves 4.

SHERBETS

Cranberry Sherbet

Cook ½ pound raw cranberries in 1¼ cups water until soft. Into container put

1 envelope plain gelatin
⅓ cup lemon juice
¼ cup boiling water

Cover and blend on high speed for 40 seconds. Add

The cooked cranberries
1 cup sugar

Cover and blend on high speed for 10 seconds. Pour into refrigerator tray and freeze, stirring occasionally. Serves 6.

Fruit Sherbet

Into container put

1 egg white
2 heaping cups finely crushed ice
3 ounces (½ can) partially defrosted fruit ade

Cover and blend on high speed for 1 minute, or until sherbet is the consistency of fine snow. Serve in sherbet glasses or, if desired, in hollowed-out orange or lemon cups. Store in freezing compartment until ready to serve. Serves 4.

Pineapple Magic

Into container put

1 can frozen pineapple chunks

Cover and blend on high speed to the consistency of a smooth, creamy sherbet. Serve immediately garnished with a sprig of mint. Serves 2.

FROZEN

Frozen Banana-Orange Cream

Into container put

½ cup hot orange juice
1 tablespoon lemon juice
1 envelope plain gelatin

Cover and blend on high speed for 40 seconds. Add

½ cup sugar
2 bananas, thickly sliced
½ cup mandarin-orange sections

Cover and blend on high speed for 20 seconds. Fold into 1 cup cream, whipped. Pour into ice-cube tray, cover, and freeze until solid.

Frozen Eggnog

In a saucepan combine 1 cup sugar, ⅓ cup water, and pinch cream of tartar. Bring to a boil and cook to soft-ball stage (136° F. on candy thermometer). Into container put

4 egg yolks
⅛ teaspoon salt
1½ ounces rum, cognac, or bourbon

Cover and turn motor on high. Remove cover and, with motor on, gradually pour in hot syrup. Chill mixture until thick and cool. Fold into 3 cups heavy cream, whipped. Turn mixture into molds or small paper cups and freeze. Makes about 6 cups frozen cream, or 18 small cups.

Lemon-Water Ice

In a saucepan combine 1 cup sugar and 2 cups water. Bring to a boil and boil for 5 minutes. Into container put

Yellow rind from 1 lemon
½ cup lemon juice
½ teaspoon ginger
Dash salt

Cover and blend on high speed for 15 seconds, or until lemon rind is finely chopped. Turn motor to low speed and remove cover. Gradually add in a steady stream the hot syrup. Pour into a refrigerator tray. Freeze 2 to 3 hours, stirring occasionally. Serves 3.

Frozen Raspberry Cream

Into container put

⅔ cup (1 small can) evaporated milk
1 thin slice lemon
1 package frozen raspberries, cut into 16 pieces

Cover and blend on high speed for 30 seconds, or until mixture is smooth. Pour into ice-cube tray and freeze. Makes 1 pint.

NOTE: Other frozen fruits such as strawberries or peaches may be substituted.

Raspberry Ice Cream

Into container put

1 tablespoon lemon juice
2 strips lemon rind
1 10-ounce package frozen raspberries, partially thawed

Cover and blend on high speed for 20 seconds, or until smooth. Remove cover and, with motor on, gradually add, in a steady stream

⅔ cup sweetened condensed milk

Turn motor off and fold raspberry mixture into 1 cup heavy cream, whipped. Turn into a refrigerator tray. Cover with waxed paper. Freeze 2 to 3 hours, or until frozen. Makes about 1 quart.

French Vanilla Ice Cream

In a small saucepan combine ⅓ cup sugar and 3 tablespoons water. Bring to a boil and boil for 3 minutes. Into container put

4 egg yolks
Dash salt
2 teaspoons vanilla

Cover container and turn motor on high. Remove cover and, with motor on, gradually pour in the hot syrup in a steady stream. Turn off motor. Fold yolk mixture into 1½ cups heavy cream, whipped. Spoon into a refrigerator tray. Cover with waxed paper. Freeze 2 to 3 hours, or until frozen. Makes about 1 quart.

French Chocolate Ice Cream

In a small saucepan combine ¼ cup sugar and ¼ cup water. Bring to a boil and allow to boil hard for 3 minutes. Into container put

1 6-ounce package semisweet chocolate chips

Cover and blend on high speed for 6 seconds, or until chocolate is grated. Push down the chocolate from the sides with a rubber spatula. Add

The hot syrup

Cover and blend on high speed for 6 seconds. Add

3 egg yolks

Cover and blend on high speed for 5 seconds, or until chocolate is smooth, stopping to stir down, if necessary. Fold the chocolate into 1½ cups heavy cream, whipped. Spoon into refrigerator tray. Cover with waxed paper. Freeze 2 to 3 hours, or until frozen. Makes just over 1 quart.

Walnut Ice Cream

Into container put

1 cup walnut halves

Cover and blend on high speed for 15 seconds, or until nuts are ground. Turn into a large bowl with 1 cup heavy cream, whipped. In a small saucepan combine ¼ cup sugar and 2 tablespoons water. Bring to a boil and allow to boil for 2 minutes. Into container put

1 teaspoon vanilla
3 egg yolks
½ teaspoon ginger
Dash salt

Cover container and turn motor on high. Remove cover and, with motor on, gradually pour in the hot syrup in a steady stream. Turn off motor. Fold egg-yolk mixture into cream and walnuts. Spoon into a refrigerator tray. Cover with waxed paper. Freeze 2 to 3 hours, or until frozen. Makes about 1 quart.

FRUIT PURÉES

Pink Applesauce

Core and coarsely cut, but do not peel 2 large or 4 small tart apples. Into container put

½ cup pineapple juice
1 slice lemon, ¼ inch thick
½ cup of the apple pieces
3 tablespoons red-cinnamon candies

Cover and turn motor on high speed. Uncover and gradually add remaining apples. Serve with sour cream and cookies on the side.

Equally good as a breakfast fruit or as an accompaniment to roast duck or goose. Makes 1 pint.

Fruit Purée

Into container put

2 cups sliced fresh fruit or berries, or 1 12-ounce package defrosted fruit or berries
1 tablespoon lemon juice
Sugar to taste (frozen fruit usually needs no sugar)

Cover and blend on high speed for 20 seconds, or until smooth. Makes 1½ cups.

Pear Purée

Into container put

½ cup water
¼ cup crystallized ginger
1 tablespoon lemon juice
1 strip lemon rind
1 medium pear, peeled, cored, and quartered

Cover and blend on high speed for 10 seconds. Remove cover and, with motor on, gradually add

3 medium pears, peeled, cored, and quartered

Cover and continue blending on high speed until mixture is smooth. Pour into sauceboat and stir in ¼ cup sugar, or to taste. Makes about 2½ cups.

Spiced-Peach-and-Date Purée

Into container put

1 package defrosted peaches
½ teaspoon cinnamon
⅛ teaspoon cloves
¼ cup sugar

Cover and blend on high speed for 10 seconds. Empty into small saucepan and add 8 ounces dates, pitted and cut. Bring to a boil and simmer for 10 minutes. This makes a thick sauce. If desired, thin with hot water. Makes about 2 cups.

Strawberry Purée

Into container put

1 pint fresh strawberries, washed and hulled
½ cup confectioners' sugar

Cover and blend on high speed for 10 seconds. Chill until ready to serve over ice cream or cake. Makes 1½ cups.

NOTE: To use frozen strawberries, blend a partially defrosted 10-ounce package strawberries and 1 tablespoon lemon juice. No sugar is needed.

HOT

Apple Pudding

In a bowl combine 1 1-pound can apples, undrained, ¼ cup sugar, the grated rind of 1 lemon, and 1 tablespoon cinnamon. Pour apples into bottom of a greased and floured 9-inch cake pan. Into container put

1 cup milk
3 ounces cream cheese
3 eggs
½ cup sugar

Cover and blend on high speed for 25 seconds. Add

½ cup flour
¼ teaspoon salt

Cover and blend on high speed for 15 seconds. Pour into cake pan over apples. Bake in a preheated 350° F. oven for 40 minutes. Serve hot with whipped cream. Serves 6.

Bakewell Tart

Spread 3 tablespoons strawberry preserve over bottom of an 8-inch unbaked pastry shell. Into container put

4 eggs
¼ teaspoon almond extract
½ cup sugar
¾ cup blanched almonds
½ cup softened butter
1 strip lemon peel

Cover and blend on high speed for 30 seconds, or until smooth, stopping to stir down if necessary. Pour into pastry shell. Bake in a preheated 425° F. oven for 25 minutes. Serve with whipped cream. Serves 6.

Chestnut Dessert

In a small saucepan cover ½ pound of chestnuts with water. Cover and boil for 20 minutes. Peel chestnuts. Into container put

The chestnuts
¾ cup water

Cover and blend on high speed for 15 seconds. Add

Dash salt
2 tablespoons soft butter
2 tablespoons cream
⅓ cup sugar
4 egg yolks
1 tablespoon brandy
1 teaspoon vanilla

Cover and blend on high speed for 10 seconds. Pour over 4 egg whites, stiffly beaten. Fold in to mix. Turn into a greased 1½-quart casserole. Bake in a preheated 350° F. oven for 35 minutes. Serve at once with sweetened whipped cream. Serves 6.

Chocolate Custard

Into container put

1⅔ cups (1 can) evaporated milk
2 tablespoons chocolate syrup
3 eggs
¼ cup sugar

Cover and blend on high speed for 10 seconds. Pour into small baking dish, place dish in pan containing about 1-inch hot water, and bake in a preheated 325° oven for 50 to 60 minutes, or until set in center. Serve with whipped cream. Serves 3.

Chocolate Soufflé

Heat ½ cup milk and 2 tablespoons butter until scalded. Into container put

1 package (6 ounces) semisweet chocolate
The hot-milk mixture

Cover and blend on high speed for 20 seconds. Add

4 egg yolks

Cover and blend for 20 seconds longer. Fold chocolate mixture into 5 egg whites, stiffly beaten. Put mixture into a 1½-quart soufflé dish and bake in a preheated 375° F. oven for 30 to 35 minutes. Serves 4.

Lemon Pudding

Into container tear

1 slice bread

Cover and blend on high speed for 6 seconds. Empty onto waxed paper and set aside. Into container put

4 egg yolks
¼ cup lemon juice
Rind of ½ lemon
1 cup sugar
¼ cup softened butter

Cover and blend on high speed for 20 seconds, or until smooth. Stir in crumbs. Fold into 4 egg whites, stiffly beaten. Turn into greased 1½-quart casserole and bake in a preheated 350° F. oven for 25 to 30 minutes, or until top is golden. Serve at once with whipped cream. Serves 6.

Orange Bread Pudding

Into container tear

2 slices of bread

Cover and blend on high speed for 10 seconds. Empty crumbs into a greased 1½ quart-casserole. Repeat, using a total of 4 slices of bread, to make 2 cups crumbs. Mix in ¾ cup seedless raisins. Into container put

2 cups milk
Thin rind from 1 orange
2 eggs
⅓ cup sugar
¼ cup soft butter
¼ teaspoon salt

Cover and turn motor on low speed. Switch to high speed and blend for 20 seconds. Remove cover and add

½ cup walnut or pecan halves

Turn off motor immediately. Pour mixture into casserole. Stir to blend and place in a pan of water. Bake in a preheated 350° F. oven for 1 hour. Serve with whipped cream. Serves 6.

Queen of Puddings

Into container tear

2 slices bread

Cover and blend on high speed for 10 seconds. Empty crumbs into a greased 1½-quart casserole. Repeat twice, using a total of 6 slices bread, to make 3 cups crumbs. Into container put

2 cups hot milk
¼ cup sugar
1 strip lemon peel
2 tablespoons butter or margarine
2 egg yolks
½ teaspoon vanilla

Cover and blend on high speed for 10 seconds. Pour over crumbs in casserole and mix well. Bake in preheated 325° F. oven for 30 minutes. Spread 2 tablespoons strawberry preserves over top of pudding. Beat 2 egg whites until foamy. Gradually beat in 2 tablespoons sugar. Continue beating until meringue is stiff and glossy. Spread over pudding on top of preserves. Return to oven and bake for 15 minutes longer, or until meringue is golden. Serves 6.

Sweet-Potato Pudding

Into container put

3 eggs
¾ cup molasses
½ cup milk
½ cup melted butter
½ teaspoon nutmeg
½ teaspoon salt
1 cup diced raw sweet potatoes

Cover and blend on high speed for 10 seconds. Remove cover and, with motor on, gradually add

2½ cups diced raw sweet potatoes

If necessary, break surface of mixture while it is blending with a rubber spatula, being careful not to dip too deeply. Pour into a 6-cup buttered baking dish and stir in ½ cup nuts and ½ cup raisins. Bake in a 325° F. oven for 1 hour, 15 minutes. Serve hot with whipped cream. Serves 6.

Wisconsin Apple Crisp

In a mixing bowl combine 1 quart peeled, sliced apples, 1 teaspoon cinnamon, ½ teaspoon nutmeg, and 1 cup brown sugar.* In container crumb, 2 slices at a time

6 thin slices bread

Empty onto waxed paper. Blender-grate ½ cup at a time,

1 cup diced aged Wisconsin cheese

Mix cheese and bread crumbs. In an 8-inch-square buttered baking dish put alternate layers of apple mixture and bread-crumb mixture, ending with layer of crumbs. Dot with 2 tablespoons butter. Bake in a 350° F. oven for 40 minutes, or until crisp and tender. Serve with cream or hard sauce. Serves 6.

* If sugar is hard or lumpy, grind it in the blender.

SAUCES

Apricot- or Peach-Rum Sauce

Into container put

1 1-pound, 13-ounce can apricots or peaches, drained
¼ cup liquid from fruit
1 tablespoon lemon juice
⅓ cup sugar
1 tablespoon cornstarch
¼ teaspoon salt

Cover and blend on high speed for 10 seconds, or until fruit is puréed. Empty into saucepan, bring to a boil, and cook, stirring, until sauce is thickened and clear. Remove from heat and stir in 2 tablespoons soft butter and ¼ cup light rum. Excellent over slices of spongecake or poundcake. Makes 2 cups.

Banana Cream Sauce

Into container put

1 ripe banana, coarsely cut
2 tablespoons brown sugar
1 cup sour cream

Cover and blend on high speed for 10 seconds, or until smooth. Good on hot spice cake or gingerbread, or on chocolate ice cream. Makes about 1½ cups sauce.

Butterscotch Sauce

Into container put

1 cup evaporated milk
¾ cup brown sugar
½ cup white sugar
2 tablespoons soft butter
1 tablespoon corn syrup
Dash salt
1 teaspoon vanilla

Cover and blend on high speed for 20 seconds, or until smooth. Makes 1½ cups sauce.

Thick Chocolate Sauce

Into container put

4 squares unsweetened chocolate, cut into pieces
1 cup sugar
⅔ cup hot milk, cream, or coffee
1 teaspoon vanilla
Dash salt

Cover and blend on high speed for 20 seconds. Store in refrigerator. Serve on ice cream and puddings. Makes a good base for chocolate drinks. Makes 1¾ cups.

Instant Chocolate Sauce

Into container put

1 6-ounce package semisweet chocolate
¼ cup hot water, milk, or coffee

Cover and blend on high speed for 20 seconds, or until smooth. Makes 1 cup.

Minted Cream Sauce

Into container put

¼ cup mint jelly
2 tablespoons hot water
1 tablespoon rum
½ cup heavy cream

Cover and blend on high speed for 10 seconds. Makes about 1 cup.

Lemon Sauce

Into container put

½ cup sugar
1 cup hot water
1 tablespoon cornstarch
Dash salt
Dash nutmeg
Outer thin yellow skin of ½ lemon
Juice of 1 lemon

Cover and blend on high speed for 20 seconds, or until peel is finely grated. Pour into saucepan and cook, stirring, until sauce is clear and thickened. Remove from heat and stir in 1 tablespoon soft butter. Makes 1½ cups.

Orange Sauce

Into container put

1 cup orange juice
Thin rind from ½ orange
2 tablespoons cornstarch
¼ teaspoon salt
½ cup sugar

Cover and blend on high speed for 20 seconds, or until rind is finely cut. Turn into saucepan and cook until thickened, stirring constantly. Makes 1 cup.

Orange-Nut Sauce

Into container put

½ cup nut meats
Thinly sliced orange rind from ½ orange

Cover and blend on high speed for 6 seconds. Add

6 tablespoons defrosted orange concentrate
½ cup (1 stick) soft butter
½ cup confectioners' sugar

Cover and blend for 30 seconds, or until smooth. Makes 1½ cups.

Strawberry Cream Sauce

Into container put

1 package defrosted strawberries
2 teaspoons cornstarch

Cover and blend on high speed for 8 seconds. Empty into small saucepan, bring to a boil, and simmer for 10 minutes, or until sauce is thick. Remove from heat and stir in ½ cup heavy cream. Makes 1½ cups.

Chapter 13 BEVERAGES

This is not a book on drinks. It is a cookbook, so we are going to treat beverages lightly. Everyone knows that an electric blender makes the smoothest, most flavorful milk drinks, malteds, double frosteds, et cetera. By adding soft fresh fruit or berries, or canned cooked fruits, additional flavor and nourishment can be added.

The one drink that everyone who owns an electric blender wants to make with *savoir-faire* is a Frozen Daiquiri, and we're going to try to tell you how. Trouble is, it is almost impossible to write the perfect recipe, for everything depends on the temperature of, not only the rum, but the ice. Ice can vary in temperature from 32° F. to many degrees below zero.

You will need a quantity of finely crushed ice. Try first to make two frozen daiquiris. Into the container put 3 ounces rum, 1½ tablespoons lime juice, and 1 tablespoon sugar. Add 2 cups crushed ice, and begin blending. If the mixture appears to be going to liquid, remove cover and add another cup of ice. If the mixture freezes so fast that the vortex caused by the revolving blades stops moving, break the surface of the mixture carefully with a rubber spatula, pulling the ice in from sides of the jar to the center. In this way the vortex will be re-created and the mixture will turn to snow. Blend for about 1 minute. You can spoon it into sherbet glasses. Sometime, for kicks, try adding a few dashes maraschino liqueur to your Frozen Daiquiri. *Salut!*

Basic Daiquiri

Into container put

3 ounces light rum
1½ tablespoons lime juice
1 tablespoon sugar
1 cup finely cracked ice

Cover and blend on high speed for 10 seconds. Makes 2 drinks.

Frozen Daiquiri

See instructions on page 261.

Fruit Daiquiri

Into container put

2 tablespoons lime juice
3 ounces light rum
1 tablespoon sugar
¼ cup canned fruit
1 cup cracked ice

Cover and blend on high speed for 10 seconds. Makes 2 drinks.

Frozen Tangerine Daiquiri

Into container put

4 ounces light rum
1 6-ounce can frozen tangerine juice, slightly thawed
2 strips lemon peel

Cover and blend on high speed for 5 seconds. Remove cover and, with motor on, add

2 cups crushed ice

Cover and blend on high speed for 15 seconds. Makes 4 drinks.

FIZZES

Golden Fizz

Into container put

1 tablespoon lemon juice
1 teaspoon sugar
1 egg yolk
3 ounces light rum

Cover and blend on high speed until very frothy. Divide into 2 highball glasses over ice cubes and fill glass with ginger ale or carbonated water.

Silver Fizz

Into container put

2 tablespoons lemon juice
2 teaspoons sugar
1 egg white
3 ounces gin or vodka
1 cup cracked ice

Cover and blend on high speed until frothy. Divide into 2 8-ounce glasses and fill glasses with carbonated water.

PICKUPS

Pineapple Pickup

Into container put

1 9-ounce can crushed pineapple
2 sprigs fresh mint
4 ounces light rum
¼ cup confectioners' sugar

Cover and blend on high speed for 10 seconds. Remove cover and add

2 cups crushed ice

Cover and blend 10 seconds, or until the mixture is smooth. Makes 4 drinks.

Pink Clam Cocktail

Into container put

¼ cup catchup
1 thin slice medium onion
1 stalk celery with leaves, coarsely cut

Cover and turn motor on high speed. Uncover and gradually pour in

2 cups clam juice

Pour into bouillon cups over an ice cube and garnish with a slice of lemon. Serves 3 to 4.

FROSTEDS

Banana Frosted

1 cup milk
1 large scoop ice cream
1 banana

Pour milk into container. Add ice cream. Cover and turn motor on high speed.

Remove cover and, with motor on, slice in banana.

Pour into large glass.

Apricot Frosted

Into container put

½ cup apricot nectar
½ cup milk
1 scoop vanilla ice cream

Cover and blend on high speed for 10 seconds. Makes 1 tall drink.

Cantaloupe Milk Shake

Into container put

1 ripe medium cantaloupe, peeled, seeded, and coarsely sliced
½ cup milk
2 tablespoons lemon juice
2 tablespoons sugar

Cover and blend on high speed for 10 seconds. Remove cover and add

About 1 pint vanilla ice cream

Pour into tall glasses. Makes 4 drinks.

Lime Nectar

Into container put

1½ cups pineapple juice
Juice of 1 lime
1 strip lime rind
¼ cup confectioners' sugar

Cover and blend on high speed for 10 seconds. Remove cover and gradually add

1 pint vanilla ice cream, softened

Blend until the mixture is smooth. Makes 4 tall drinks.

Mocha Smoothee

Into container put

1 tablespoon instant coffee
2 teaspoons sugar
3 tablespoons chocolate syrup
2 scoops chocolate ice cream

Cover and turn motor on high. Remove cover and, with motor on, gradually add

1½ cups milk

Pour into tall glasses. Makes 2 drinks.

Orange-Cream Freeze

Into container put

1 cup orange juice
2 scoops vanilla ice cream

Cover and blend on high speed for 10 seconds. Pour into 8-ounce glasses. Makes 2 drinks.

Orange-Pineapple Smoothee

Into container put

1 cup orange juice
2 slices fresh or canned pineapple
1 thin strip rind of 1 orange
1 scoop vanilla ice cream

Cover and blend on high speed for 10 seconds. Makes 2 drinks.

Pineapple-Banana Smoothee

Into container put

1½ cups pineapple juice
½ cup dry-milk solids
1 ripe banana, sliced

Cover and turn motor on high. Uncover and, with motor on, add

2 scoops vanilla ice cream or pineapple sherbet

Pour into tall glasses. Makes 2 drinks.

Strawberry-Orange Frosted

Into container put

1 cup orange juice
1 10-ounce package partially defrosted strawberries

Cover and turn motor on high. Uncover and, with motor on, add

2 scoops vanilla ice cream

Pour into tall glasses. Makes 2 drinks.

MILK

Apricot Flip

Into container put

1 cup milk
½ cup cooked apricots
½ cup cracked ice

Cover and blend on high speed until smooth. Pour into 8-ounce glasses. Makes 2 drinks.

Banana Flip

Into container put

1½ cups milk
2 strips orange rind
Dash salt
⅛ teaspoon almond extract
1 tablespoon honey
1 large banana, peeled and quartered

Cover and blend on high speed for 20 seconds. Chill. Makes 2 drinks.

Mocha Float

Into container put

1½ squares unsweetened chocolate, cut into pieces

Cover and blend on high speed for 6 seconds. Add

¼ cup boiling water

Cover and blend on high speed for 6 seconds. Add

2 teaspoons instant coffee
3 tablespoons sugar
Dash salt
1½ cups cold milk

Cover and blend on high speed for 15 seconds. Pour into 2 tall glasses and top with scoops of vanilla ice cream.

Prune Flip

Into container put

1 cup milk
4 pitted cooked prunes
¼ cup prune juice
1 teaspoon honey

Cover and blend on high speed until smooth. Pour into 8-ounce glasses. Makes 2 drinks.

Raspberry Flip

Into container put

1 scoop raspberry sherbet
½ cup milk

Cover and blend on high speed for 20 seconds. Makes 1 tall drink.

Strawberry Blonde

Into container put

1 cup fresh strawberries
1 cup milk
1 cup cracked or crushed ice
1 tablespoon sugar, or few drops non-caloric sweetener

Cover and blend on high speed for 10 seconds. Pour into tall glasses. Makes 2 drinks.

FRUIT

Cranberry Cocktail

Into container put

1 cup cranberry juice
1 tablespoon lemon juice
1 egg white
½ cup cracked ice

Cover and blend on high speed for 20 seconds, or until frothy. Makes 2 drinks.

Grapefruit Cooler

Into container put

1½ cups grapefruit juice
½ cup orange juice
¼ cup confectioners' sugar

Cover and turn motor on low speed. Switch to high speed and blend for 10 seconds. Remove cover and add

1 heaping cup crushed ice

Cover and blend for 5 seconds. Makes 3 tall drinks.

Orange-Apricot Nectar

Into container put

2 cups orange juice
3 tablespoons lemon juice
½ cup cooked apricots
1 cup cracked ice

Cover and blend on high speed until smooth and frothy. Makes 4 drinks.

Orange Spooner

Into container put

1 6-ounce can frozen-orange-juice concentrate, partially thawed
Thin strip lime rind
¼ cup confectioners' sugar
2 sprigs mint

Cover and blend on high speed for 10 seconds. Remove cover and add

3 cups crushed ice

Cover and blend until mixture is smooth. Serve with spoons. Makes 4 "drinks."

Pineapple-Water-Cress Cocktail

Into container put

2 cups pineapple juice
2 cups water-cress leaves
3 tablespoons sugar or 2 teaspoons honey
½ cup lemon juice
1 cup cracked ice

Cover and blend on high speed for 20 seconds. Makes 6 drinks.

Tomato-Juice Cocktail

Into container put

1 slice medium onion
1 thick slice green pepper
1 teaspoon celery salt
¼ cup parsley clusters
¼ teaspoon orégano
Dash Tabasco

Cover and turn motor on high speed. Uncover and, with motor on, gradually pour in

3 cups tomato juice

Chill and serve cold garnished with lemon slice. Makes 6 drinks.

Watermelon Punch

Into container put

Juice of 1 lime
1 cup orange juice

Fill container to top with

Chunks of seeded watermelon

Cover and turn motor on high. Remove cover and, with motor on, drop in more watermelon chunks until liquid in container reaches almost to the top. Pour into goblets over crushed ice and garnish with mint. Serves 6.

NOGS

Cranberry Nog

Into container put

½ cup cranberry juice
½ cup cream
2 teaspoons sugar
1 egg
½ cup crushed ice

Cover and blend on high speed for 10 seconds, or until frothy. Makes 2 drinks.

Eggnog Sherbet

Into container put

2 tablespoons sugar
1 egg
2 ounces bourbon
2 tablespoons heavy cream
2 cups crushed ice

Cover and turn motor on high. Uncover and stir surface of mixture with a rubber spatula until mixture is consistency of fine snow. Spoon into sherbet glasses, or store in freezing compartment. Makes 2 "drinks."

Velvet Nog

Into container put

6 eggs
1 cup hot milk
¼ cup sugar

Cover and blend on high speed for 5 seconds. Pour into bowl and stir in

½ cup brandy
1 cup heavy cream

Makes 6 drinks.

COFFEES

Hot Mocha

Into container put

1 cup hot coffee
¼ cup chocolate bits
½ cup heavy cream

Cover and blend on high speed for 20 seconds. Serve in cups. Makes 2 drinks.

Coffee Nectar

Into container put

1¼ cups strong cold coffee
2 scoops coffee ice cream
Dash cinnamon

Cover and blend on high speed for 20 seconds. Makes 2 drinks.

Coffee Punch

Into container put

½ cup strong cold coffee
½ cup cognac
2 tablespoons sugar
2 cups milk
½ cup heavy cream

Cover and blend on high speed for 15 seconds. Pour into punch glasses and sprinkle with freshly ground nutmeg. Makes 4 drinks.

Coffee Tropicale

Fill container half full of crushed ice. Add

4 teaspoons sugar
1½ cups strong cold coffee

Cover and blend on high speed for about 1 minute, or until thick and creamy. Pour into glasses. Makes 4 tall drinks.

HOT

French Chocolate

Into container put

1½ squares unsweetened chocolate, cut into pieces

Cover and blend on high speed for 6 seconds. Add

¼ cup sugar
Dash salt
2 cups hot milk

Cover and turn motor on low, then on high speed for 15 seconds. Pour into cups and top with whipped cream. Makes 3 drinks.

Hot Rum Punch

Into container put

3 lemons, sliced and seeded
½ cup sugar
1 teaspoon ground ginger
1 pint light rum

Cover and blend until lemon is finely chopped. Strain into warm punch bowl. Add

1 pint cognac
1 pint sherry
1 quart boiling water

Serve in mugs or punch glasses. Makes 16 drinks.

Tom and Jerry

Into container put

2 eggs
2 tablespoons sugar
2 ounces blended whisky or rye
2 ounces dark rum
1½ cups milk

Cover and blend on high speed for 10 seconds, or until very frothy. Empty into saucepan and heat, but do not boil. Serve in hot mugs with a topping of grated nutmeg. Makes 4 drinks.

MISCELLANEOUS

The Dietini

Into container put

10 ounces evaporated milk
8 ounces pineapple juice
6 tablespoons dextrose
2 tablespoons corn oil
½ cup brewers' yeast

Cover and blend on high speed for 20 seconds. Chill and drink 4 ounces 5 times daily. About 930 calories. Makes 20 ounces.

Meal in a Minute

Into container put

¾ cup orange juice
1 egg yolk
1 tablespoon honey wheat germ

Cover and blend on high speed for 20 seconds. Makes 1 tall drink.

INDEX